Daily Pivots

Breaking Free from Habits That Hold You Back

◆ ◆ ◆

Gerry Fisher
Life & Career Coach

Dan,
Thanks for being
supportive of my
writing!

Gerry Fisher

◆   ◆   ◆

ISBN: 9781521354155

❖   ❖   ❖

Change is the only constant in life. — Heraclitus

Everybody thinks of changing humanity and nobody thinks of changing himself. — Leo Tolstoy

◆　◆　◆

To my amazing husband, David Kimble.

Though results often vary, you inspire me to be my best self. I can't imagine a greater gift. *Thank you!*

Table of contents

Acknowledgements..xi

Forward.. xv

Do I have to read the whole thing? xviii

What's with that writing style? xxi

PART I: PLEASE GIVE ME SOME BACKGROUND 1

Chapter 1: Let's look at goals...3

A story about goal setting...5

Goals are building blocks for your vision 10

Goals should be observable and measurable........................ 13

Skills are needed to achieve goals smoothly 16

What gets in the way of reaching goals? 19

Let's sum it up.. 22

Chapter 2: Let's look at habits..25

A story about habit change 27

How habits work..31

Changing habits...38

Inflection points 42

Keystone habits...44

Willpower..47

How long it takes to form a new habit 49

Let's sum it up..54

Chapter 3: Let's look at motivation..............................57

A story about motivation 59

How does motivation work?..64

How focus affects motivation.....................................68

How to use motivation well 69

How to jump start motivation.....................................75

How to "slip into a groove" without motivation 79

How fear and depression trump motivation 85

Let's sum it up...90

Chapter 4: Let's look at change................................95

A story about change...97

The TTM stages of change 101

The role of structure...................................... 106

The role of conversations................................ 110

The role of social environment 114

The role of trial and error 118

The role of habits... 122

Let's sum it up.. 125

PART II: JUST GET TO THE POINT ALREADY! 127

Chapter 5: Let's look at Pivot Points...................... 129

Defining pivot terms..................................... 131

"Has the jury reached a verdict?"...................... 133

Using the Courtroom Drama Pivot Story 139

Let's sum it up..145

Being patient..149

Boosting confidence..165

Calming anxiety and fear..183

Changing unhelpful beliefs..203

Competing..221

Enjoying the journey of life..227

Focusing..239

Letting go of control..261

Making decisions..275

Managing anger..289

Reducing jealousy..295

Relaxing about mistakes..299

Taking better care of yourself..315

Trying something different..331

Appendix A: Let's look at mindfulness.. 339

   Mindfulness exercises.. 340

   Mindfulness teachers.. 342

Appendix B: Let's look at thinking habits.. 345

   Thought Stopping 345

   Don't apply "mood gasoline" 346

About the author.. 355

Endnotes... 357

Acknowledgements

Daily Pivots helps people to stay on track and to complete long-term projects, such as taking a few years to write a book like this one. During that time, I've been bolstered by the work, love, and support of a large number of people. Although I won't succeed at mentioning everyone here, please know that you are all deeply appreciated.

Let me start by thanking all my past and present clients. You've been brave and trusting enough to allow me into your private worlds. I've learned so much from you, and both my private and professional lives are better as a result. From the bottom of my heart, thank you.

Next, my Life & Career Coaching practice follows in the footsteps of giants in the counseling and writing fields. My deepest thanks go out to (in no particular order) Marsha Linehan; David Burns, M. D.; Margot Fanger; Charles Duhigg; Joan Borysenko; Edward Hallowell, M. D.; Jeffrey M. Schwartz; Amy Johnson, Ph.D.; and Byron Katie. Even though I've never met any of you, it feels as if you and your work "have my back." Deepest respect and regards to you.

Thanks go out to my first counseling supervisor, Mary Arrigo. Before I could be an effective change agent for clients, I needed to learn how to form an initial, personal connection. You helped me to build those foundational skills for sitting with people, listening to them, and related to them. You have my deep appreciation.

Many thanks go out to Dave Griffin, Peter Hurley, and the dearly departed Frank Willison. You folks gave me the professional trust and support I needed, so I could make a living during my transition to counseling and coaching. Your helping hand is greatly appreciated. Additional thanks go out to all the super-bright, fun, and talented professionals I met while working in high-tech, first at Digital Equipment Corporation and later at SiteScape, with special shout outs to Lori Kay Brown, Mary Utt, and June Lemen.

Thanks go out to my reviewers who helped me write a better book. Your feedback was invaluable, Genie Arnot and Paula Kozak (*shut UP!*). Also, thanks go out to my talented and supportive artist, Elizabeth Gething; her emotional support was as terrific as her artwork.

Family and friends have been *incredibly* supportive while writing this book. Thanks go out to my mom, Helen Fisher, my sister, Judy Watson, her husband, Tom Watson, and my fantastic nieces and nephews, Sam, Audrey, and Rose. Warm thoughts go out to my Aunt Claire Pileski, who is no longer with us. She always underscored her rock-solid support with a quick joke, big smile, and hearty laugh. I miss her so.

Let it be noted that my husband, David Kimble, started this whole thing a few years ago by saying to me, *It's time to write your book.* I replied, *But I don't know what I want to write about.* He said, *So?!* Thanks for the loving nudge, husband.

Finally, let me thank a guide, friend, and colleague whose presence in my life has been immense. There'd be no career—never mind a book—without the influence you've had in my life, Dennis Young. For decades, you were a combination wise uncle, fun older brother, and strategic partner. To quote a Paul McCartney song, *I can't tell you how I feel / My heart is like a wheel / Let me roll it to you.* Thanks so much, Dennis.

Forward

Allow me to tell a brief story that explains why I wrote this book.

For 30 years, I lived in and near Boston, Massachusetts. My former home is *fantastic* in many ways, but it can be a *horror show* when it comes to traffic. The joke is that its roads were designed in the 1600s for cows and horses, not cars. It's a labyrinth of one-way streets, narrow passage ways, and almost nothing resembling a grid. In response to this mess, I found myself often embroiled in road rage.

When it comes to stressed-out driving, much of it is clearly Boston's fault, *not mine.* Yet, blaming the city and other drivers didn't make me feel any better, and my angry driving was frustrating my passengers. *So, I decided to make a change.*

I'd been practicing mindfulness meditation for years, and I often taught it to my Life & Career Coaching clients. One of the many benefits of this wonderful practice is stress reduction.

Clearly, it was time to practice what I preached. So, I vowed to dedicate myself to becoming *Mr. Zen Driver*, feeling relaxed no matter what the Traffic Gods threw my way. This personal project wouldn't be earth shattering; it would just be a nice, minor adjustment to my daily life.

Almost right from the start, I noticed that I was jacking up my own emotional intensity while driving. For example, without realizing it, I'd made a sport out of judging other drivers, which created a constant stream of negativity. Also, I was mentally pushing, as if my judgment of bad drivers could *shame them* into driving better. Finally, I noticed that I'd almost always leave for an appointment with *juuust* enough time to arrive, and then I'd lose my cool if I was delayed.

So for a year or two, I practiced adjusting my attitude and forming some new habits: leaving for an appointment ten minutes early, driving in the middle lane on the highway to avoid both the speed demons and slowpokes, and leaving room for people to cut in front of me.

I made steady progress, and my driving became more and more pleasant for all involved. Yet, my self-improvement project still felt like a tedious slog, requiring focus and lots of effort over time. That is, until I made an interesting breakthrough.

One day while highway driving, I noticed a car nudging up against my lane ahead of me, so I slowed down to give the driver room to do something stupid. As soon as the car lurched in front of me and cut me off, I felt a brief surge of anger. Then almost at the same time, this thought entered my mind: **No harm, no foul.** Instantly, my muscles relaxed, I eased back into my seat, and calmness blanketed me.

*Wow! What just **happened**, there?*

"No harm, no foul" is a term I learned during pickup basketball games played without a referee. It's an agreement to continue play unless the bump or slap prevented you from scoring. *Let's let the little things go and just enjoy the game.*

Many years of playing pickup ingrained that lesson in me, and applying it to my driving created a very quick emotional *pivot*, allowing me to avoid the bad habit of losing my temper and to shift instead into a more accepting, easy-going manner. This emotional "change of direction" happened in an instant, and it rippled *immediately* into better driving.

*   *   *

Now, what would it take to skip years of tedious habit change and jump right to the rapid success of "No harm, no foul"? What would it take to cement that change into a new set of habits?

Having helped hundreds of Life & Career Coaching clients to make changes in their lives, I've observed what's led to avoiding the trap of bad habits, getting quicker and easier results, and making significant breakthroughs. This book is the result of what I've learned; it's my professional *secret sauce*.

Do I have to read the whole thing?

Daily Pivots is about breaking free from unhelpful habits that hold you back from making important changes you want: examples of change include switching careers, saving more money, losing weight, or starting your own business. Use all the other great Self Help books out there to get custom tips and guidance for your specific goal; use this book at the moment you're struggling with your commitment and need to get back on track emotionally.

If you want to jump right in and try it, skip ahead to Part II, and start with the *Let's look at Pivot Points* chapter. Then, pick a few of the Pivot Inspiration stories that follow to apply to your situation.

Pivot Inspirations are organized by the unhelpful habit that's pushing, tugging, or bullying you off course. For example, if you're facing a situation in which you usually lose your temper, then try using a story in the *Anger management* chapter to help you pivot into a calmer state; if you're a chronic people pleaser or an over-the-top caregiver, then try the stories in the *Taking better care of yourself* chapter to help you pivot into giving yourself what you need before assisting others.

Of course, effective change involves more than just pivoting. It's helpful to have a vision and a set of supporting goals, an understanding of how habits both support and undermine your change efforts, a sense of how to work with your desire for motivation, and some ideas for managing your environment as you implement your change project.

If you benefit from this type of background information, then read the four chapters in Part I before learning to pivot.

Here are brief descriptions of what you'll find in the rest of this book:

- *PART I: PLEASE GIVE ME SOME BACKGROUND*

    - *Chapter 1: Let's look at goals*—Describes how to design and pursue goals, and what can block your efforts.

    - *Chapter 2: Let's look at habits*—Explains how habits work, their power, and how to change them.

    - *Chapter 3: Let's look at motivation*—Discusses when motivation is helpful and when it's beside the point.

    - *Chapter 4: Let's look at change*—Covers additional challenges you'll face during any large change effort.

- *PART II: JUST GET TO THE POINT ALREADY!*— Provides the tools you need to perform daily pivots.

    - *Chapter 5: Let's look at Pivot Points*— Helps you understand the use of Pivot Inspirations to avoid unhelpful habits and to swing instead toward the change you want.

The remaining chapters are organized by the unhelpful habit you want to overcome.

- *Being patient*

- *Boosting confidence*

- *Calming anxiety and fear*

- *Changing unhelpful beliefs*

- *Competing*

- *Enjoying the journey of life*

- *Focusing*

- *Letting go of control*

- *Making decisions*

- *Managing anger*

- *Reducing jealousy*

- *Relaxing about mistakes*

- *Taking better care of yourself*

- *Trying something different*

- *Appendix A: Let's look at mindfulness* discusses a skill that can help you slow down, observe, and better recognize opportunities to pivot.

- *Appendix B: Let's look at thinking habits* introduces thinking patterns that increase feelings of hopefulness, calm, and manageability, thereby increasing your confidence when pivoting.

WHAT'S WITH THAT WRITING STYLE?

To assist you while reading, let me review a few decisions I made about how to present information in *Daily Pivots*.

First, I generally use gender-neutral terms. Even so, writing "she or he" too often slows things down. For that reason, I often alternate examples randomly between female and male subjects. Please understand that these examples can apply to someone of any gender.

Second, I mention a few stories about my Life & Career Coaching clients. To protect their privacy, I've blended the stories of more than one client, offered no real names, and altered other identifying details. As for the stories about me, I tend to spill my guts...within reason.

Third, I use yin-yang symbols to represent how it feels to be pulled in two different directions at the same time. During big or complex change projects, people often get stuck in this way.

Here's an example of how I use these symbols:

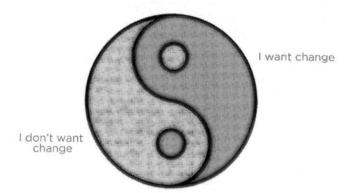

Daily Pivots helps you let go of feeling the need to choose one side or the other. Instead, think through how both sides are true, relax about it, and find a way to move forward in a way that honors both sets of feelings and desires. For example, many people both "want change" *and* "don't want change." Recognizing and working with both feelings is necessary for getting unstuck and successfully completing your change project.

Fourth, *Daily Pivots* makes frequent use of the term *Self Talk*, which is the process most of us use to think through a situation. It could be as simple as a quick thought (*No harm, no foul*), or it can be as involved as telling ourselves a story or having an ongoing conversation with ourselves. Self Talk is a powerful tool you can use to think things through and to make better decisions over time.

Finally, I footnote references to other books. You can find the footnotes in the *Endnotes* section at the end of *Daily Pivots*.

◆ ◆ ◆

PART I: PLEASE GIVE ME SOME BACKGROUND

If you're a no-nonsense, just-get-to-the-point kind of person then...well...*what are you doing here?* Get your butt over to *PART II: JUST GET TO THE POINT ALREADY!* (page 127) so you can start pivoting.

Now that we got rid of *them*, let's talk.

The Daily Pivot method is about getting where you want to go in the *short run*. For example, you set out to write your resume or complete your online dating profile, and you feel the pull of procrastination (*Let me just check my email first*) or the avoidant push of fear (*What if I mess it up?*). Right in that moment, you need to pivot away from the unhelpful habit and toward more productive action.

Of course, these daily adjustments are happening within the context of your larger change project. Before learning about pivoting, it can be helpful to review change theories and approaches that can help you get where you want to go in the *long run*.

For example, you may have wondered why your change efforts feel so hard today when they seemed so easy last week. You may have observed that it's easier to change when you have the vocal support of a group of people around you. Not surprisingly, the *lack* of support from those around you, never mind outright disapproval, can feel like a weighty burden. Finally, you will most likely run into the desire to strike a deal with the devil by putting off what you have to do until you feel more motivated...and then days, months, and even years can pass.

Managing these challenges as you master *Daily Pivots* will increase your likelihood of success.

Here are the chapters in Part I:

- *Chapter 1: Let's look at goals*—Describes how to design and pursue goals, and what can block your efforts.

- *Chapter 2: Let's look at habits*—Explains how habits work, their power, and how to change them.

- *Chapter 3: Let's look at motivation*—Discusses when motivation is helpful and when it's beside the point.

- *Chapter 4: Let's look at change*—Covers additional challenges you'll face during any large change effort.

PART II: JUST GET TO THE POINT ALREADY! explains how to pivot and provides Pivot Inspiration stories for you to try. Find the ones that work best for you, and use them as models for developing your own Pivot Inspirations.

Chapter 1: Let's look at goals

Daily Pivots is about learning skills for *staying on track* with the change you want. Nonetheless, it's helpful to start the discussion by exploring how to *get on track in the first place*.

To begin, it can be helpful to understand a basic process for setting and reaching goals. Some of the most worthwhile goals in life—changing a career, completing a degree, planning for retirement, or starting a new business—need to be broken down into smaller steps, prioritized, adjusted according to your willingness to actually do them, and completed in order over time. Applying a helpful structure to your goal setting can greatly improve the quality of your results for these very important projects.

This chapter presents:

- *A story about goal setting*—Provides a helpful case scenario.

- *Goals are building blocks for your vision*—Describes how to structure and prioritize your goals.

- *Goals should be observable and measurable*—Provides tips for creating well-formed goals.

- *Skills are needed to achieve goals smoothly*—Highlights approaches that make goal attainment more efficient.

- *What gets in the way of reaching goals?*—Explains why excellent goal setting is often not enough.

- *Let's sum it up*—Summarizes goal setting before moving on to discuss habit change.

The next section presents a story about how I got it together financially as a way to highlight important aspects of goal setting.

A STORY ABOUT GOAL SETTING

At the very end of a recession in 1983, I graduated from college with a degree in English Literature and Computer Science. For one year afterward, I worked in retail before transitioning to a well-paying job as a software technical writer.

I remember what a joy it was to stop living like a student. For example, I no longer had to pull my shopping cart to the side of the grocery store before approaching the cash register, doing some quick math and putting back a few items that I couldn't afford. I remember how good it felt to retire those old, plastic milk crates and to buy a real bookshelf. Finally, for the first time in my life, I was able to buy my own car.

Life was good.

At the beginning of my career, my employer had a stock-purchasing program that offered a 20% match for the amount of money I saved. A finance-savvy friend of mine told me, *Even if you buy the stock and sell it immediately, you make an instant 20% profit with no risk. It's like free money.*

Who could say no to free money, right? So, I decided to participate. Every six months the program purchased new stock for me, and I immediately sold it all and pocketed the money. *Sweet!*

Eventually, in my mid-20s, it occurred to me that it might be a good idea to put away some of this money. I mean, I understood already how handy it would be to have a stash set aside for emergencies such as an unexpected, expensive car repair. So, given that I grew up in a financially unsophisticated, lower-middle-class family, I began to save the only way I'd seen my parents do it: when I had some extra cash, I deposited it into a savings account at the bank.

Well, the better part of a decade came and went, and in terms of savings, I didn't have much to show for it. To summarize my approach, I deposited the amount of money I felt like saving, and I did so when I felt like it. Then, I withdrew money when I felt the need. In the end, I was left with only a few hundred dollars in my account.

Oooops. No savings.

Soon after I began my first ever live-in relationship, I received mail from a financial planning firm. Thinking they might have a better strategy for saving money, I set up a meeting.

The financial planner began by asking me to create a vision of my life ten years into the future. At that time, I imagined I'd be married to my current partner and living in a split-level ranch in the suburbs of Boston. It was a conventional dream: house, lawn, white picket fence, mini-van.

The planner also asked me very detailed questions about my lifestyle—travel, vacations, taste for material objects, plans for children—to get a sense of how much it would all cost. Then, she asked some questions about how I imagined my retirement, ran some calculations, and came up with a reasonable prediction of how much money I would need in order to live comfortably when my career ended.

After our first meeting, my planner presented a written report that included *very specific* recommendations, which I accepted and put into action. In brief summary, there'd be one pot of money that would eventually be a down payment on a house and another pot to be used for retirement. Finally, my planner helped me set up direct deposit, so that we added a specific, affordable amount to my investments every pay period. As an added benefit, direct deposit made it difficult for me to save less or to withdraw money—I'd have to go through my financial planner to make these adjustments.

In my very early 30s, I was finally getting my financial act together. *It felt great.*

In short, the plan worked. Although I'm still working on the finer details of retirement, I was able to use one set of savings

 to place a down payment on a house approximately a decade after I began investing.

The ultimate success of the house purchase isn't the most interesting part of the story. As they say, life is what happens to you while you're busy making other plans, right?

First, my relationship status changed a few times in between making the plan and purchasing a house. I had been operating under a very strong-yet-fuzzy belief that I needed to be with a partner before purchasing a home. So, when my relationship dissolved soon after making my financial plan, it took some years to meet my next partner, settle down, and create enough joint savings to buy property.

Second, the purchased house didn't look like my original vision. Instead of the suburban split-level, it turned out to be a condo in a two-family home, which was located in a city almost adjacent to Boston. No yard, picket fence, or mini-van. Instead, I had affordability, restaurants within walking distance, and quick and easy access to the city.

Third, there were other circumstances that influenced how well I managed to save. In the early years, I sold some stock to buy a home computer (which *seemed* like a good idea at the time), and I wasn't the most attentive investor, relying completely on my financial planner to make suggestions. I also never increased the amount I saved, even though I'd been receiving annual raises at work.

Since the house purchase, we've sold that property, and we've moved from Boston to Baltimore and purchased another home. Also, we're continually updating our vision for retirement.

In conclusion, this story is typical of goal setting in that, once you've reached your end point, you don't stay satisfied for long. Pretty much, you turn right around, start dreaming again, and set new goals. While you're still drawing breath, it never ends. This is a *good* thing.

*   *   *

This story isn't a perfect model either for financial planning or for goal setting. Still, it's helpful in the way it highlights both ineffective and effective goal setting. For example, notice:

- The difficulty of saving money when I didn't have a reasonable vision as to how I was going to spend it. Goals need to be emotionally anchored in a sense that, with each output of effort, you're getting closer and closer to getting something really good that you want.

- How, over time, my vision for the future changed. If I'd postponed setting goals until I was 100% certain about my future, I'd have been much older before I bought my first property. A vision is vital for getting you off the couch, stoking motivation, and getting you moving. However, it's not all that important that your end point match your initial vision.

- The difference between "I'm going to put money into my savings account whenever I have extra cash," and "I'll put $300 into my investments every pay period." Establishing a clear amount ($300) and a specific timeframe (every pay period) were absolutely critical to saving money successfully.

- That some habits of mine—automatic ways I behaved, thought, made decisions, and believed—slowed down my process. I failed to save during my initial years as a professional just because I habitually relied on a savings account. If I had purchased a condo while single, I could have made significantly more profit much quicker from my real estate dealings, but I was too much in the habit of thinking that I should be in a relationship before I built a home for myself. Most habits are wonderfully useful, yet some habits can be the biggest—often invisible—roadblocks to success.

This chapter discusses in greater detail how to form goals and work effectively toward reaching them. The next section provides more detail about the relationship between your future vision and action you should be taking now to begin working toward it.

GOALS ARE BUILDING BLOCKS FOR YOUR VISION

When people work on personal projects that unfold over significant time—finding a compatible partner, developing a career, or starting a new business—it's helpful to organize the effort. In general, you want to have a strong sense of your end goal, or in other words, why you're going to be working so hard for so long. Also, it can help to prioritize your efforts so that you have a sense of what needs to be done earlier rather than later.

When potential clients ask about Life & Career Coaching, I often say that we Life Coaches create a *strategic plan* for people's *personal lives*, and we help people to stay focused, accountable, effective, and motivated as they put the plan into action.

While working for a Fortune 500 computer company back in the 1980s, I took part in a handful of strategic planning exercises, and they can be quite involved. Formal strategic planning often guides people through the process of creating a mission statement, discussing strategies, developing a detailed set of goals and objectives, authoring a formal plan, and thorough discussions about the difference between "tactics" and "goals" and "tasks." *Phew!*

When it comes to Life Coaching, I like to keep things simple. My clients usually want to lose some weight or save money to buy a house; they aren't looking to run a major, multinational corporation that employs many thousands of people.

Given the smaller size of the projects, here's a good, basic strategic planning process you can use for personal goals:

1. Use your imagination to develop a clear, detailed vision of your life after completion of your project.

2. Get a sense of some goals you'll need to complete in order to make your vision a reality.

3. Get a sense of the order in which the goals might best be completed, creating priorities for your project.

4. Complete the goals one by one, and **adjust your plan and vision over time**, as you learn more by doing.

As demonstrated by the previous financial planning story, it's not unusual for a plan or vision to evolve over time. For example, I had envisioned buying a house in the suburbs of Boston with my partner, and, by the time I'd saved a down payment, I had a different partner and bought a house near a city. As you strive to complete goals—reaching some and failing to complete others—you learn more than you knew when you began, and the process helps you adjust your original plan for the better. You should modify plans over time, sometimes tweaking them a little bit, and other times giving them a complete overhaul.

Those of you who have created professional strategic and project plans may notice that "get a sense of goals and priorities" is a bit vague, and that part of the project often involves more detailed planning. For example, it can be helpful to distinguish between *long-term goals* as opposed to *short-term goals*. A good Life Coach can assist a client with more of these details as well as with creating well-formed, effective goals.

In conclusion, I'd like to bring your attention back to *the vision*. When I hear goals discussed in the mainstream media, I notice people paying far too little attention to the importance of vision. Most goals are individual steps in a journey that leads to a destination, and it's *the desirable destination* that motivates you to *make the effort today*.

When imagining your vision, paint a picture, tell a story, and use your imagination to make it as complete and specific as possible. Understand that there are no right or wrong details to put into your vision. So...*just make it all up*. It's an enjoyable possibility, not a commitment.

Try to imagine what you look like after the vision becomes real, how do you feel, what thoughts cross your mind, who's keeping you company, where are you, what are you doing, and what will you enjoying most about finally arriving at your destination?

With a *clear vision*, it becomes easier to create *clear goals* needed to produce the results you want. In addition to having a clear vision, there are other approaches that can boost the effectiveness of creating, prioritizing, and working toward goals. The next section provides tips for creating well-formed goals.

GOALS SHOULD BE OBSERVABLE AND MEASURABLE

There are many wonderful discussions, blog posts, tools, and tips available that can assist with goal setting. For example, search the Internet for the excellent *SMART* goal-setting acronym. Yet again, in the interest of keeping it simple, this section provides only a few of the most vital things to remember.

First, make sure that your goals are *observable* and *measurable*. If someone can't see you complete a goal, or if you can't assign a number to your results, then redefine you goal until it meets those criteria.

For example, "I want to be happier" is not a well-formed goal, because it's a personal feeling left completely up to your own reporting. If you go back to your vision, apply some creativity, and flesh out specific details, then you can determine exactly what activity is likely to result in feeling happier. For example, people who end up in a deeply happy place might have started their own businesses, lost weight, found a compatible partner, bought a home, and so on. Perhaps your vision reveals that it's a *combination* of these goals that are likely to produce your happiness.

Just to clarify the process, let's take one vision and map it to observable and measurable goals. For example, some people might have a vision that a slimmer body would result in feeling healthier and happier. Given that, the following would be well-formed goals:

- *I will lose 20 pounds between January and the start of summer.*

- *I will go to the gym three to four times a week.*

- *I will complete at least 30 minutes on the elliptical machine each time I go to the gym, all the while keeping my heart rate in the Cardio heart-rate range.*

Someone could see you at the gym four times during the week, or could wander by the elliptical machine and see your heart rate register in the Cardio range, so these goals are *observable*. You can weigh yourself in mid-June to determine if you've lost 20 pounds, and you can grip the handles on the elliptical machine to determine your heart rate, so the goals are *measurable*.

Also, consider starting with small goals and working your way toward larger ones. Given the exercise examples, it's possible to hurt yourself if you go for too much, too soon. For example, maybe doing 15 minutes of an elliptical workout in the Weight Loss range is a wiser place to start; if you begin with an initial goal that was too easy, you can always increase it later. If you find yourself unwilling to do a short-term goal, then go back to the thinking-and-planning stage, and come up with a short-term goal that you are more likely to complete; a completed mediocre goal is better than an awesome goal left undone.

Remember that your goals are single steps in a larger, longer journey. This is an effort you're making to please yourself. So, *what's the rush*, right? Slow and steady more often wins the race.

At the beginning of your projects, don't forget to set goals for conducting some research. With my Life & Career Coaching clients, I'm frequently advising them to venture out and get more information before launching expensive or wearying efforts.

Although Internet, library, and book research efforts are all helpful, set more goals that involve "picking the brains" of other people who are knowledgeable about your project. For example, if you want to lose 20 pounds before summer, sit down over coffee or lunch with a few people who've already lost a substantial amount of weight and kept it off, or talk to someone with expertise about the subject: a personal trainer, a nutritionist, a Health & Wellness Coach, or someone who works in sports medicine.

Seeking information from knowledgeable people is a form of *networking*. A thorough discussion of networking is beyond the scope of this book. Though, if you'd like a quick description about how to get started, you can read a posting in my *Getting to Clear and Present* blog about the topic (http://tinyurl.com/informational-interviewing).

Finally, as I say to my clients, none of us have a crystal ball that makes predictions about the future, so it's best not to expect a *perfect* plan at the beginning of a project. Be patient and tolerant about using "trial and error." If a goal is a spectacular failure, chuckle about it, analyze it, and try something else based on what you've learned.

Perfection isn't the point. The point is to stay active, learn, and adjust as you go. One area of learning involves using and improving *skills*. Skills aren't just knowledge, but the ability to take effective and consistent action in pursuit of your goals. The next section discusses skill building in more detail.

SKILLS ARE NEEDED TO ACHIEVE GOALS SMOOTHLY

A client of mine recently asked why some people are better than others at setting, working toward, and reaching goals. Great question...let's explore it.

This section reviews some of the skills that help people reach goals as smoothly and efficiently as possible. In no particular order, consider this short list:

- **Patience**—As mentioned previously, goals are small steps in the much larger journey of making your vision a reality. For example, saving to buy a house took a decade for me to complete. Building a new business can take from many months to years before you see profit. Learning dating skills and finding a compatible partner can take months to years.

- **Ability to *delay gratification*—**This skill is a specific kind of patience that results in maintaining committed action for potentially long periods of time before getting any satisfying rewards. For example, when saving money to buy my first house, I needed to be able to put money away every paycheck for a decade—and tolerate the ups and downs of the stock market—before getting enough results to feel intense excitement.

- **Ability to commit—**At its heart, *commitment* means that you follow through and do something simply because you said you would. Put another way, you are a woman or man of your word. Feelings will come and go, wax and wane, but you follow through and take the action because that's the kind of person you intend to be.

- **Willingness—**This skill means being open to taking necessary action unconditionally. For example, there are times when you are motivated, when you're clear about honoring a promise, and those feelings drive your action. Then, there are other times when you're willing to *just do it* regardless of how you feel in that moment; you're willing to do what works.[1]

  The opposite of being willing is to be *willful*, which is a refusal to take necessary or helpful action until personal conditions are met. Willful people dig in their heels, make demands or bargain, make their actions dependent on their moods, rationalize, criticize, or sit on their hands instead of taking helpful, necessary action.[2]

- **Imagination**—Given that a clear vision leads to clear, attainable goals, it's helpful to have enough imagination and creativity to conjure the specifics of your desired future.

- **Curiosity**—During a long project, you might not be clear about your next step, a goal might fail, or it could produce unexpected results. Curiosity is fuel for the engine of critical thinking. For example, when my goal of settling down in the suburbs fell through, I needed to become curious about other living situations that might please me.

- **Critical thinking**—Because trial and error is an important part of adjusting your goals, it's helpful to be able to be curious and to analyze why something did or didn't work. After this analysis, you can use what you learned to create better, more effective goals in the future. Your personal project benefits from a *learning curve*.

- **Interpersonal skills**—Some of the best information available about your project can come from people who have already been there and done that. So, it's helpful to be able to approach these people, ask for time to talk, and conduct a useful conversation. Also, partnering with people can help you achieve goals faster, and it can be critical to enroll your friends and family in support of your goals.

- **Ability to maintain focus**—When I troubleshoot goal setting with my clients, sometimes the problem is that they forget or get distracted. It's critical to maintain a gentle, consistent focus on both the overall vision and the Goals for This Week, on both where you want to be in the future and what you need to do about it today.

- **Flexibility**—Given that goals don't always produce expected results, and given that your environment might not consistently provide needed resources, it's helpful to be flexible. Are you willing to apply trial and error? If life blocks you from completing one goal, can you shift gears and work on another one until you can return to your original plan?

Remember that not everyone has an equal amount of all of these skills. Yet at the same time, *everyone has the ability to learn, to practice, and to develop skills.* As is the case with all types of skills, *consistent practice* is critical for improvement. The next section reviews ways in which we fail to practice new behaviors consistently, which threatens both our skill level and our ability to reach our goals.

WHAT GETS IN THE WAY OF REACHING GOALS?

OK, so let's say you've got yourself a clear vision of what you'd like to accomplish. You've got a good sense of some long-term and short-term goals. You've done some planning, so you understand goal priorities. Finally, even though you might not have completely mastered all the skills that make reaching goals easier, you're generally on board with the idea of being patient, delaying gratification, staying focused, and being flexible enough to adjust your plan as you go.

So, now you'll execute your plan and reach all your goals without any problem, right? *Right?*

I know. Me neither. Let's explore some missing pieces to the goal-setting puzzle.

First, we're *emotional creatures,* not just logical ones, so having the most brilliant plan is not enough. You need to align your feelings in support of your project. Second, we're also *creatures of habit,* and habits can overwhelm and undermine logical plans.

This mix of emotional nudges and pushes, possibly combined with a set of Thinking and Doing habits, can present itself in strong patterns. The following is a list of a few of these patterns, some of which are likely to be very familiar:

The Procrastinator knows when she's procrastinating. She can tell you what she usually avoids, when she avoids it, and what she does instead to distract herself. The Procrastinator often would like to feel motivated before getting on with it, but she strongly senses that the old Nike commercial was right, and that she should stop waiting to feel like it and *just do it.* And she *will* just do it...right after she cleans the bathroom or reaches the next level in her video game.

The Perfectionist takes on too much, obsesses over unimportant details, takes criticism way too personally, and blurs the line between what he does and who he is. He's often very bright and verbal, because he was a perfectionist in school. So, he's able to give you a very logical, true argument about why he doesn't *need* to chase a crazy level of quality. However, when faced with choices in the moment, he feels compelled to get it not just right, but *perfect.*

The Righteous Avenger places more value in being right than in getting the job done. Concepts such as *justice, right and wrong,* and *fair and unfair* take up a significant amount of space in her head. She knows that walking in other peoples' shoes, collaboration, tolerance, and picking her battles would lower her stress level and get the job done quicker, easier, and better. But *not* if it means accepting that she might be wrong or allowing others to get more than their fair share.

The Emotion Junkie longs to be understood and to get what he wants, but he goes about it by venting how he feels. He's truly the King of TMI (too much information). Also, the Emotion Junkie comes in subcategories: The Rage-aholic, The Love Addict, The Over Sharer, the Feel-My-Pain-Or-Else Bully. He can point to strained relationships and trouble caused by his behavior. But it's the fault of all of those people *who just don't understand him* or how *he feels.*

These common patterns of behavior aren't the end of the story; the ways in which our emotional states and habits derail our logical plans are endless. For example, people who struggle mightily with resumes *know* that they can hire a resume writer or consult a good resume book. Smokers *understand* the damage that they are doing to their lungs and are *aware* that their early death would hurt their family members. People in debt *know* the basics about balancing a checkbook and making a budget.

So, right in that moment when we feel pulled in the wrong direction by an unhelpful emotion or set of habits, *what can we do?*

First, the information in *PART II: JUST GET TO THE POINT ALREADY!* provides information about how to detect that moment of weakness, plant a foot, and swing back in the direction of executing your plan. Learning when and how to pivot well is the key to avoiding the lure of unhelpful habits.

Second, the next few chapters contain information that helps you understand how to manage habits, and how to boost your emotional state from *"I'm just not feeling it right now"* to *"OK, I'm willing to honor my commitment and git 'er done."*

The next section reviews topics discussed in this chapter and gives you some food-for-thought before moving on to the next chapter.

LET'S SUM IT UP

Strategic planning—creating a vison and a set of goals to bring it to life—can be very deceptive. On its surface, it appears as if the main point is to be *organized*, but there's something more important happening on a deeper level.

Consider how simple it all sounds. First, imagine a clear vision of success: for example, feeling established in a great new career, marrying a wonderful spouse, or enjoying your fit body. Then, set goals, commit to completing them one at a time, and work regularly to stay accountable. Repeat until your vision becomes a reality.

BOOM! Drop the mic and walk away.

...or maybe not.

On the one hand, being organized can greatly assist your project. However, let's circle back to a point made earlier in the chapter as a way to tease out additional challenges. Your goals need to be emotionally anchored in a sense that, with each step, you're getting closer and closer to *getting something* **really good** *that you want*.

If you're seeking an ice cream at the corner store, there's no chance that you'll lose sight of why you're walking a block. If you're longing for a compatible spouse, yearning for a career change, or trying to save money to buy a house, there's more opportunity over time to deviate from the plan.

The remaining chapters in Part I help you understand what it takes to stay on track during long-term projects. The next chapter explains how habits can be both your best friends and worst enemies while working toward change, and what you can do to adjust unhelpful habits.

Chapter 2: Let's look at habits

To complete a large change project, you need to prioritize and accomplish smaller goals until the change is complete. If unhelpful habits run counter to daily goals, your change will be shaky and brief. Think of habits as being stones that make up a rock-solid foundation; once that foundation is in place, you can build your house—*lasting change*—on top.

At its heart, *Daily Pivots* is all about *habit change*. You can look at pivoting as resisting the automatic pull of *the old* and creating an automatic pull toward *the new*. So, before you attempt to adjust them, it's helpful first to understand how habits work.

Most of the material in this chapter is inspired by a wonderful book entitled *The Power of Habit: Why We Do What We Do in Life and Business*, by Charles Duhigg, which discusses habits of individuals, successful organizations, and societies. In addition to being thorough and thought provoking, Duhigg is an entertaining story teller. This book impressed me so much that I buy a copy for every one of my coaching clients. Please do consider buying and reading this wonderful, helpful book.

Daily Pivots references the information in *The Power of Habit* that discusses individuals' habits, which is important for pivoting. I also recommend that you buy the book if you are a business leader or social activist; it provides a wealth of fascinating information about those topics, which are outside the scope of *Daily Pivots*.

This chapter presents:

- *A story about habit change*—Provides a helpful case scenario.

- *How habits work*—Describes the mechanics of habits, why they are useful, and why they are so hard to change.

- *Changing habits*—Provides tips for modifying an existing habit or creating a new, more powerful one.

- *Inflection points*—Explains how creating plans for dealing with adversity can assist habit change.

- *Keystone habits*—Explores how not all habits are alike, and how some have an interesting ripple effect.

- *Willpower*—Describes how willpower itself is a habit with some interesting characteristics.

- *How long it takes to form a new habit*—Helps to set some expectations for habit change.

- *Let's sum it up*—Summarizes habit change before moving on to discuss motivation.

The next section tells a story about my efforts both to gain weight and to lose it, and it presents examples of how habits work and the challenges we face while attempting to maintain new, better habits.

A STORY ABOUT HABIT CHANGE

Let's start the story a few years back. At that time, I was solidly middle aged, and like many men at that stage of life, I'd gained more belly weight than I liked. Despite my dissatisfaction, years passed when I hadn't felt compelled to do anything about it. After all, there were *plenty* of men who had bigger bellies, and mine wasn't *that* big, right?

Then came the illusion-shattering holiday season of 2013 when I was given two pairs of pants. Receiving this gift was delightful...*trying them on was not.*

You see, my loved one had purchased the correct size but neglected to buy *the stretch waist.* As a result, I could manage to squeeze into one pair, but they were so tight I couldn't breathe; I couldn't even button the second pair. I was *embarrassed*, man!

After years of ignoring the problem, I made a quick and firm decision: *I'm **not** going up a waist size. I'm going to lose this belly.*

So, in the early months of the New Year, I worked to put a gym routine into place, and I embarked on what I called my Belly Reduction Program. Within three or four months, I'd lost  approximately ten pounds, which was enough to fit into both pairs of new pants. Although there was more work to be done, I felt delighted at the relatively short time it took for me to see some initial results.

Now, let's flash back to the year 1979, my senior year of high  school. At that time, I'm 6'5" and weigh 145 pounds. My classmates joke that I'm a refuge from a famine-ravaged land. As shown in the yearbook picture to the left, there's no part of my tank-top uniform that touches my bony frame as I come down after shooting a layup, only air puffing up the shirt.

I'm *skinny*. And I'd remain very thin for the first few decades of my adult life.

Flash forward more than two decades to the late 1990s. I'd just ended my second long-term relationship, and I'd finished a very challenging master's degree in a counseling field. I'd been working both a full-time job and an unpaid internship, studying like crazy, eating poorly, and neglecting my health.

After taking a summer off after graduation, I made a quick and firm decision: *I'm going to get in shape. While I'm at it, I'm going to build some **muscle**.*

So, I embarked on a dedicated gym routine for three or four years, developed an average build, and eventually increased my weight from 170 pounds to 210 pounds. It took several years of weight lifting before the first signs of success. While swimming at a family outing, my sister glanced at my shirtless torso and said in a dry, matter-of-fact tone, *You have shoulders now.* I indeed had shoulders...and some arms and a bit of a chest.

After I reached my end-goal of getting into shape and developing some muscle, I fell off my gym routine, visiting the gym sporadically for a few months before abandoning it altogether for up to a few years at a time. On again briefly, and off again, it would take the Shock and Awe of the ill-fitting-pants episode approximately a decade later to motivate me to return to the consistent work of staying in shape.

*   *   *

As you can tell from this story, I've been on both sides of the weight divide, having been both underweight and overweight. There've been years when I was in the habit of eating healthy foods and staying active, and years when those habits fell by the wayside.

On the one hand, I won't bore you with everything it took to get nutrition and exercise habits up and running. On the other hand, I want to share a few interesting observations made during my on-again-off-again experiences.

For example, dropping my first gym routine after I'd gained enough muscle highlights the importance of having a vision that drives daily commitment, which is the foundation for creating a new habit. I'd gained my muscle and arrived at my vision, so why keep going, *right?*

To return to consistent gym attendance, I needed a new, motivating vision: *fit into my new pants and avoid the embarrassment of going up a waist size.* Now that I've reached *that* end-goal, I'll have to develop another vision to keep going. Perhaps this will work: *keep my cholesterol low and set the stage for being healthy into retirement.*

As an example of a seemingly minor-yet-interesting detail, my longest and most dedicated times at the gym involved attending health clubs that had a hot tub. I noticed that I would often boost my motivation on tough days by focusing on how good it was going to feel soaking in the tub after my workout. It was my *reward* for toughing it out.

As a final example, I noticed that my current Belly Reduction Program seemed to coincide with changing other habits in my life. Shortly after getting back to the gym, I found myself flossing more regularly, making my bed consistently, frequently meditating, and more. There was something about getting back to the gym that made other changes easier.

Eight months into my Belly Reduction Program, I read *The Power of Habit: Why We Do What We Do in Life and Business*, by Charles Duhigg. Not only were my story and experiences common for any human being trying to make changes in life, but they were remarkably typical in terms of how habits work. Specifically, the book helped me to understand why my fitness efforts succeeded and failed at various times throughout the years.

Also, given very recent information about how short-term weight-loss efforts don't work well[3], and how efforts need to be measured in terms of *years* and not weeks or months, it's helpful to be clear about forming solid habits and knowing how to keep them in place over the long haul.

As I present information about habit change in the rest of this chapter, I'll refer to details about the Belly Reduction Program to illustrate key points. The next section breaks down habits into their parts and shows in detail how they work.

How habits work

Back in the mid-90s when I first started counseling people, I began my investigation into exactly what was blocking people from reaching their goals. At first, I thought that people didn't have a good strategy and plan for success, but I soon discovered that I was wrong.

Very often, people knew *exactly* what they needed to do, and could describe their clear intentions with conviction. Yet, as they ventured back into their lives, they encountered intense thoughts and feelings that derailed them. The trick, it seemed, was helping them to reduce or eliminate the thoughts and feelings that kept interrupting their efforts.

Over time, I found a number of techniques that fell into the category of *emotion-management skills* or *cognitive-behavioral techniques (CBT)*. All of these skills involve some combination of slowing down, clearing the mind, being able to focus strongly on the present moment, and thinking and speaking using phrases that are soothing, which enabled clients to relax and refocus on their objectives instead of on their upset.

At first, the process seemed simple. I teach, the client learns, and the skills get applied when needed. *Simple.*

Well, I first saw this approach fail when a client with panic disorder described how deep breathing techniques didn't reduce her attacks, even though research tells us that this approach works. I asked her to describe what happened, and she said, *I felt the panic attack coming on, I got short of breath, I tried deep breathing, and it didn't work.* I asked, *How often did you practice deep breathing before the panic attack occurred?* She replied, *I didn't.*

I'd forgotten to emphasize *practice.* As a former jock, I knew the value of practice. I was used to completing a drill time after time after time in practice sessions. Then during a game, I could act automatically and quickly without having to think. And it's not just sports. People become skilled at public speaking by practicing giving speeches, someone becomes great at knitting by making a lot of sweaters and booties, and great cooks are the result of cooking and cooking and then *cooking some more.*

So, urging my clients to practice emotion-management skills helped, but I've found recently that it's more helpful to describe it as the need to *build helpful habits*, including habits of thought, behavior, and focus. In the same way that a great chef is in the daily habit of focusing on all things cooking, people with strong emotional dispositions are in the daily habit of focusing on all things emotionally smooth, strong, and healthy. Habitual use is critical; you can't put the skill on a shelf for five months, pull it out during an emergency, and expect it to work.

*　　*　　*

Let's get technical for a few moments.

We've known for a long time that repeated behavior during habit formation causes a sequence of neural synapse activity in the brain to become optimized.[4] Yet, it's been only within the last 15 years or so that we've been able to understand in more detail which parts of the brain are involved in habitual behavior and what that has to do with how habits work.

In very brief summary, we hadn't understood the extent to which a habit causes the brain to shut off and go on automatic pilot. In other words, "when a habit emerges, the brain stops fully participating in decision making."[5] Also, older theories about habits included the idea that you can eliminate a bad habit. We now know that habits can be ignored, changed, or overridden by stronger habits; however, old habits never completely go away.[6]

Much of *Daily Pivots* provides techniques for ignoring the siren call of an unhelpful habit. Nonetheless, for now, let's focus on two other ways to address an unhelpful habit: change the existing habit, or form a new one that will be stronger and more compelling than the old habit. To accomplish either of these tasks, it's helpful to break a habit down into its parts so as to understand their functions.

33

Consider the following:

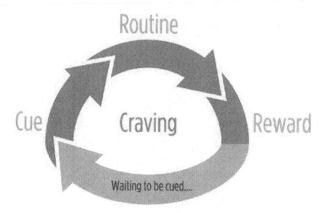

A habit starts with a *cue*, which triggers your brain to go on automatic pilot to start the behavior. The *routine* is the actual behavior. The *reward* is a positive result you get from having taken the action. The *craving* creates an anticipation that drives the routine. This is often called a *behavior loop*, because the satisfaction of the reward strengthens the power of the cue; looping over time, the behavior becomes more and more automatic, and the habit gets stronger and more ingrained.[7]

Note that the brain does not distinguish between "good" and "bad" habits.[8] You're cued, the higher-functioning parts of your brain ramps down (you stop making decisions), you act automatically, and you receive your reward. *Done deal.*

OK, now let's apply this process to my gym workouts, which were described at the beginning of this chapter:

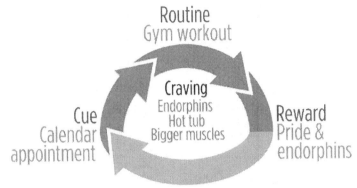

When the time arrives for my scheduled workout, I'm cued to begin my routine. I grab my gym bag, walk downstairs, and go to the gym. When I'm finished with my workout, I feel proud that I honored my commitment and worked hard, and I feel the exhilaration of the endorphins pumping. There are a few aspects of the gym that create anticipation for more. As mentioned at the beginning of this chapter, thinking about soaking in the hot tub is very motivating. Feeling the rush of endorphins and seeing the pumped-up muscles after weightlifting also generate excitement, enthusiasm, anticipation, and craving.

Notice that cravings are often more sensual and, well, *sexier* than the rewards; reflect on how different it feels to desire a long-term goal versus craving something in the moment. Notice also that losing weight isn't a reward that I receive immediately from a single workout; that's a reward I receive over time. Therefore, I'd better be getting something satisfying out of the gym workouts until the weight loss starts to show.

As one final note about how habits work, it's important to remember how quickly you lapse into a habit. The cue results in a very quick start to your routine, and the completion of your routine results in a rapid sense of reward. Also, when the habit involves an emotional reward, the total elapsed time of one go-round of the habit loop can be measured in milliseconds.[9] This dynamic is in play when we're cued by fear and seek anxiety relief; the *relief* is the reward.

Before moving on to the next section, which discusses how to change habits, let's take a closer look at some implications of how habits work:

- Habits disconnect your behavior from reason (logic) and memory, and they operate separately from decision making. They truly put you on *autopilot*. For example, if someone confronts you about a bad habit and asks, *What were you thinking?*, the most honest answer would be, *I wasn't*. The parts of your brain that you normally use to think, make decisions, and choose are turned off during a habitual routine, making it very hard to choose another behavior in that moment.

- Given the mechanics of habits, there are biological reasons why it's hard to change when an old habit is standing in the way. During your change project, I recommend that you resist any urge to criticize yourself harshly. It's not that you have some massive character flaw; it's more likely that you're just being typically human. The normally helpful automatic nature of habits makes it challenging to modify the "bad" ones.

- When you're faced with a troublesome habit, *speed is an enemy*. Anything you can do to slow down your thinking and acting will assist in your attempts to tinker with your habits, giving you an opportunity to ignore or change them. (*Daily Pivots* will discuss the benefits of slowing down throughout the chapters in Part I.)

- It took repeated action over a long period of time to create the habit, so give yourself some time to alter it and to form new habits.

- New habits are created *every day*; don't dwell on the false notion that habit change is impossible.

- If you think of all the work and time needed to create the new habit, it can seem too difficult. The next few sections of this chapter will give you more hope for rapid change. In addition, here's a tip for getting started: for now, focus on slowing yourself down, and try to identify the cue and reward for your habit. Focus on *understanding your habit* before you attempt to *change it*.

- On the one hand, habit formation requires consistency; you need to respond to the cue, do the routine, and feel the reward frequently in order for the action to become an automatic habit. On the other hand, studies have shown that the consistency doesn't have to be daily.[10] Working on a new habit three, four, or five days a week will get you there in good time. Taking a day off once in a while is fine. Just don't take three or four *months* off. Rest up briefly, and then get back on track with developing your new habit as soon as possible.

The next section provides practical advice about what you can do to change an unhelpful habit.

CHANGING HABITS

It's important to remember that habit change usually requires experimentation and time. Understanding that, let's take a look at the basic formula for changing an existing habit. As a summary of the thorough description provided in *The Power of Habit*[11], you need to:

1. Identify the cue and reward for your habit.

2. Swap the troublesome routine for a more helpful one.

3. Repeat using the new routine in response to your cue over a long enough period of time to change the habit.

Usually, people want to swap out the routine of a "bad" habit and put in a "good" routine. Nonetheless, let's use the habit diagram from the last section to illustrate this process in terms of my Belly Reduction Program.

Let's review the following:

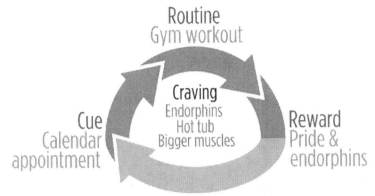

Now, let's say that I can no longer afford my gym membership. I'm left with an existing cue and a desired reward, minus a routine and any associated craving, as follows:

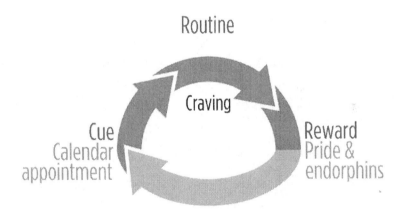

Let's say that I decide to try jogging as my new routine, and I select a tree-lined path that winds through a park as my running course. My planned habit modification can look like this:

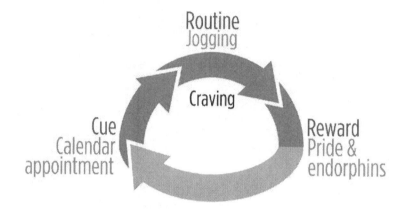

So, day after day, week after week, when I'm cued by my calendar, I change into my jogging clothes, go for a run, and feel a sense of accomplishment in terms of better endurance, distance improvements, and stick-to-it-iveness during days when I feel low motivation. Also, I'm well aware of the exhilaration of the endorphins pumping immediately after my run. Over time, my jogging routine becomes easier to maintain, and it becomes more and more of an automatic habit.

Automatic habits usually involve an anticipation or craving. Perhaps my new exercise regime produces these types of cravings:

The Power of Habit provides a number of examples of replacing "bad" habits with "good" ones. My favorite is Duhigg's description of how he changed his "buy a cookie at the cafeteria mid-afternoon at work" habit, which is described in the e-book version.

During my Belly Reduction Program, most of my activities involved creating new, stronger habits that felt more compelling than the old ones. However, there was a replacement involved in my snacking habits. My old habit was *cued* by hunger, involved the *routine* of eating chips, and the *reward* of getting my concentration back and *relief from hunger*; I tended to *crave* salty snacks. Keeping the cue and reward in place, I replaced the chips with a small handful of nuts, and one low-calorie appetite suppressing candy, and it tended to work beautifully. The nuts were even able to satisfy my salt craving.

Recently, I've noticed that my old habit of binging on chips returned, and this happened during a time of stress[12] in my life. First, I noticed the return of the old habit very soon. Second, I recommitted to eating nuts and an appetite suppressing candy instead. With a few days of renewed focus and commitment to my newer habit, I was back on track.

The next section discusses seizing an opportunity for habit change.

INFLECTION POINTS

Long-term change isn't supposed to happen perfectly and smoothly. *Five steps forward, two steps back, three steps forward, one step back....* The trick is to avoid letting those backward steps discourage you; recognize the backsliding as soon as possible, and refocus on returning to the forward steps.

The *Power of Habit* describes a very useful framework for working through difficult times and potential setbacks. People who anticipate a moment of pain or difficulty, create a plan for handling it, write down the plan, and frame their activity around cues and rewards fared much better with creating habits than those who did not plan. The anticipated moment of pain is called an *inflection point*.[13]

When working with my Life & Career Coaching clients, I emphasize having *contingency plans*. That's just a fancy way of describing the anticipation of potential problems, and working out a few ways of addressing the problems should they occur. When a client sets a specific goal for a given week, you can think of it as Plan A. Plan B, the contingency plan, comes into play if something blocks Plan A.

Using my Belly Reduction Plan as an example, I pulled a calf muscle on the tread mill eight months into my efforts. My Plan B was to continue going to the gym, eliminate all aerobics, do light stretching of my calves, do my core exercises (for stomach and back), and focus on weight lifting. I executed that plan for 10 days, re-evaluated my calf, determined that I had recovered, and then returned to aerobic workouts at that time.

As another example, all of my snacking can be seen as planning for an inflection point. When I get hungry in between meals, I plan on having a small handful of nuts and an appetite suppressing candy (Plan B), a protein bar (Plan C), or a protein shake (Plan D). Because I have these contingencies in place and locate these snacks at work and at home, I'm able to avoid vending machines, convenience stores, chips, and fast-food drive-through windows.

Finally, the entire *Daily Pivot* approach is a program designed to manage inflection points. Skim the chapters in *PART II: JUST GET TO THE POINT ALREADY!* Each of these categories describes an inflection point common when embarking on large change projects: losing your temper, being intimidated by competition, feeling afraid, struggling to make a decision, and more. When you experience one of these inflection points, your plan is to pick up this book and read the Pivot Inspiration that provides you with emotional relief from the troubling situation. After you experience relief, you can more easily pivot back toward the change you want.

The next section describes types of habits that achieve broader, quicker, and sometimes delightfully unexpected change.

KEYSTONE HABITS

If we reviewed in detail all of the new behaviors involved with my Belly Reduction Program, it all might seem intimidating. Implementing a gym routine involves many of what I call *mini-habits* that support the larger effort. Mini-habits for my Belly Reduction Program include tasks such as packing a gym bag, having snacks available at work and at home, using the calendar to cue workouts, shopping regularly for healthy foods, making sure that gym clothes are washed and available in a timely fashion, establishing and adjusting exercise routines, having an energy drink ready for my workouts, and more.

For example, if I had to examine the cues and rewards for each mini-habit, experiment with new routines over time, and consciously commit to doing these new routines daily, then I would probably fail. That would require an *overwhelming* amount of thought, focus, and effort.

As discussed previously, one way to make a long-term project feel more manageable is to implement just a few mini-habit changes at a time; in other words, implement your change program *incrementally*. But what if there was a way to trigger a bunch of habit changes with a single effort, making large-scale change much easier?

Well, *there is* such a way.

A *keystone habit* is a routine that, if put into place, can trigger broad changes either for an individual or throughout an organization.[14] Everyone has one or more keystone habits that will produce such a ripple effect, and different habits may work for different people. Still, research has determined that certain keystone habits seem to work for most of us. Of course, be ready to apply a trial-and-error approach to discover which keystone habits work best for you.

One theory about the ripple effect of keystone habits focuses on the general process for making complex changes over time. When you embark on a project such as my Belly Reduction Program, you invoke commitment, structure, planning, willpower, an ability to delay gratification, and more. Also when you successfully put into place a keystone habit, you've created a *small win* that makes other changes feel more do-able.[15] Your belief in your ability to change increases dramatically, and you tend to act with renewed confidence.

Although some keystone habits involve complex projects, there are a few of them that are fairly straight forward, perhaps even *easy* to implement. Also in case you were wondering, we don't always have a logical explanation as to why a particular keystone habit works.

Using my Belly Reduction Program as an example again, here are some habits completely unrelated to fitness that seemed easy to implement at the same time as watching my nutrition and getting back to the gym: meditating, flossing, making my bed, and keeping up with my business blog.

It just so happens that creating an exercise regime is a common keystone habit for individuals.[16] (I didn't know this when I began my own program.) To give you a feel for other keystone habits, here are a few intriguing ones described in *The Power of Habit*:

- Making your bed every morning, which is linked with better productivity, a greater sense of well-being, and a stronger ability to stick with a budget.[17]

- Eating dinner together as a family, which is associated with children having better homework skills, higher grades, better emotional control, and more confidence.[18]

- Food journaling.[19]

- Willpower.[20]

The stories in *The Power of Habit* bring to life the notion of keystone habits. If you are in a leadership position, I highly recommend reading the book to understand how you can apply the concept of keystone habits to a company or an organization, which is beyond the scope of *Daily Pivots*.

Willpower is a particularly important keystone habit, and the next section describes some of its unique qualities.

WILLPOWER

Willpower is a unique keystone habit, in that it's exercised and used to build every other habit. Yet, given what we know about willpower, we have to use it carefully.

So, let's start by taking a look at all of the skills that you enhance and activate as you practice and boost your willpower:

- Being more easily able to perform a task regardless of how you feel

- Being able to resist temptation

- Delaying gratification, creating an ability to "play the long game"

- Strengthening your focus, increasing your ability to maintain it over time

- Fostering an ability to make and keep commitments

Circling back to my Belly Reduction Program, my weight-loss routine exercised and strengthened all of these willpower skills. I needed to go to the gym regardless of my motivation or energy level, I needed to resist temptations (fast food, pizza, starchy carbohydrates, chips, blowing off the gym), I needed to stick to my weight-loss program for weeks before I saw a significant improvement, I needed to pay attention to my cues and how well I was executing my routines (*did I pack my gym bag and include my energy drink?*), and I needed to restart and tweak my program week to week in a consistent and committed way.

Now, using willpower sounds so good that you might be tempted to ram into place a slew of new habits using force of will.

Please don't.

The Power of Habit provides some fascinating and helpful information about the limits of willpower, which can help us determine when and how to use it effectively. Consider the following:

- Willpower is a learnable skill[21], so don't fret if you feel that you're lacking. You can build willpower with consistent practice over time.

- Think of willpower as you would a muscle. It's very powerful, but when used continuously over time, it weakens and needs rest before it can perform again at its maximum capacity.[22] For example, if you are going to call upon your willpower in the evening, make sure that you haven't drained it too much throughout the day. If you need to exert willpower for a task, try not to schedule that effort at the same time another activity is demanding your willpower; prioritize and space out your change efforts.

- When people are treated with kindness and respect before being asked to exert willpower, they tend to perform the task at a higher level, and they end up with more of it in reserve afterward. For example, if people are given a sense that they are in control or that their efforts will benefit an ally, they show an increased ability to exert willpower to perform the task well.[23] This would explain why negative thinking inhibits wellbeing and emotional health, which is an example of an individual not treating herself with kindness and respect. Negative thinking saps willpower that could be used for productive, goal-oriented action and for creative problem solving. It's like trying to perform well under the thumb of a vicious task master. (See *Appendix B: Let's look at thinking habits* for more information about reducing negative thinking.)

Now that we've discussed how habits work and how habit change can be maximized, let's move on to the next section, which provides information you can use to set reasonable expectations about the length of time needed for your change effort.

HOW LONG IT TAKES TO FORM A NEW HABIT

It's a frequently asked question by my Life & Career Coaching clients, and it's a very difficult one to answer: *How long will this take?* One fact that makes this question difficult is that everyone brings a different set of goals, skills, levels of support, and challenges. Also, the overall change effort often depends upon a person's ability to form mini-habits in support of the larger goal. Despite these facts, requesting a timeframe for change is reasonable and a worthwhile topic for discussion.

So, let's begin by focusing on some research about habit change.

How long does it take to form a new habit?

21 days, give or take. At least that's the word in Self Help circles. However, there's more to the story.

Being in the business of helping people to change, I was startled when I realized that there was a three-or-four-week timeframe being held up as a standard for habit change. Now on the one hand, I've noticed some patterns in my work about how long it takes clients to see results and how long it takes for the results to look firm. On the other hand, I haven't seen *any results* by the vast majority of my clients that take place in three or four weeks.

A really terrific column by Oliver Burkeman shed some light on the amount of time it takes to form a new habit. Burkeman states that the three-or-four-week estimate comes from an observation by Maxwell Maltz, a plastic surgeon and best-selling author who noticed that it took amputees an average of only 21 days to adjust to the loss of a limb. Therefore, any adjustment or change can be accomplished in 21 days, right?[24] *Well, not so fast...*

Burkeman does a terrific job of explaining why this logic is flawed and why habit change can take different lengths of time for different people. He makes the very valid point that habits—even "bad" habits—are responses to needs (rewards). He gives the example that, if you're eating junk food to meet the need of providing comfort during stressful times, then attempting to replace the habit with healthy eating will fail to meet the need of "comfort."[25] The change won't take. Burkeman is pointing out the importance of correctly identifying a cue-reward pairing before attempting to replace a troublesome routine.

Another excellent column, this one by Gretchen Rubin, cites Burkeman. She makes the point that a study done in the 2000s found that participants took 66 days to create a new habit. However, she discusses how the length of time can depend on the person and the type of change being made. Finally, the study showed that daily repetition is not necessary; missing a day here and there did not seem to affect the success rate or the time it took to form a new habit.[26]

To add to the research, let me share some observations I've made over the years about the rate of change for my clients. Even though people meet with me either weekly or every two weeks, I haven't seen a significant difference in the rate of change based on the frequency of meetings. With consistent and committed effort by my clients, I see habit change beginning to occur at the three-month mark (90 days) and getting very firm near the six-month timeframe (180 days).

Let me provide a little bit more detail.

At approximately the three-month mark, my clients experience *some movement*; sometimes it's significant, and sometimes it's a small amount. At this time, the ways in which my clients have felt "stuck" are starting to loosen, and my clients feel more capable—experiencing less fear, procrastination, confusion, and negativity. Also, they've begun to make progress toward their larger goal of finding a partner, changing jobs, losing weight, starting their own business, and so on.

After they've experienced that initial progress, some clients decide to continue on their own without further coaching. Others feel tentative and are concerned about backsliding. The second group usually decides to stay with me for an average of 6 months, until new habits are firmer and the end of the project feels closer.

Now, despite the fact that I've given you some numbers, you may think that there's no telling when a habit will become fully formed. *You'd be right.* Having said that, here are some things to keep in mind when evaluating the length of time to expect for habit change:

- The quicker you can move from thinking and planning into action, the quicker you'll be able to form your habit. *Chapter 4: Let's look at change* discusses a model for looking at the change process and tips for moving through the various stages of change.

- Remember that habits require consistent repetition. Working on your habit five days a week often gets quicker results than working on it once a week, though once a week can be effective for many types of habits. Taking a break on weekends or taking a mental health day now and then won't greatly affect progress. Now imagine working once a month, once a season, or once a year; those rates are too infrequent.

- When progress slows down, we lose sight of small wins, and we can lose motivation and give up. The next chapter goes into greater detail about the role of motivation in the change process.

- Remember that, if you put down a project for a long time, it can take a while for you to get back into the groove when you come back to it. Whereas, if you leave it for a day and then come back, it's relatively easy to pick up where you left off. To help yourself get back on track with your habit-change project as soon as possible, consider using the *Highway rumble strips* Pivot Inspiration in the *Relaxing about mistakes* chapter in *PART II: JUST GET TO THE POINT ALREADY!*

- Consider identifying a keystone habit. If you can make progress on quitting smoking, exercising, building willpower, playing a musical instrument, and so on, then it may create a ripple effect, making other habit changes quicker and easier.[27]

- Sometimes change can happen quicker with a little bit of external motivation in the form of social support. Notice that many Self Help programs, including Weight Watchers and 12-step programs, emphasize group meetings. Involving groups and other people in your change process can provide structure, accountability, reassurance that you're being assisted by a power greater than yourself, and an increased belief that the change will be successful.[28]

- As mentioned, old habits never completely go away, and they can reappear in times of stress.[29] When viewed from this angle, it calls into question whether you're ever 100% done; maintenance is ongoing. Even automatic habits need continual repetition to remain dominant and automatic.

The next section reviews topics discussed in this chapter and gives you some food-for-thought before moving on to the next chapter.

LET'S SUM IT UP

Often when hiring me to be their Life & Career Coach, clients say they want help *getting unstuck*. The idea is that a part of them really wants to produce a positive, new effect in their lives, but something else is slowing them down, holding them back. When describing that "something," the conversation can get very intensely negative and unhelpful.

For example, they'd love to change, but they're *lazy*, you see. Or there's this chemical imbalance that keeps producing wildly unhelpful moods that get in the way. Perhaps it's attention deficit (though clients often say, *I tried medication, but it didn't seem to make a difference*). Maybe the problem is that they inherited their depressive or anxious dispositions. Or perhaps they just don't have what it takes to succeed, or maybe the problem is imbedded in their personality.

But what if none of those conditions is the *major* factor keeping them stuck and unable to move forward? What if they are reasonably normal, healthy, skilled, and capable human beings who just happen to have some *unhelpful habits* that keep getting in the way? What if they could view these habits as benignly as we view **lots** *of habits*, such bouncing a leg, twirling hair on a finger, frequently saying *ummm*, or cracking knuckles? No big deal, but a change would be nice.

I like that an emphasis on habit removes the impulse to criticize ourselves so brutally. Because habits can be changed or overridden by other habits, emphasizing them helps my clients to focus on *practicing and learning*. You wouldn't verbally attack someone for something they haven't learned yet, right?

Finally, I find that I can help clients to make sometimes *amazing progress* if I can get them to view "thinking" and "emotional reactions" either as being habits or their byproducts. Pivoting is the act of detecting old Thinking and Doing habits, having Self-Talk conversation, and convincing yourself to begin practicing new Thinking and Doing routines that are more likely to get you want you want.

You can learn to focus and draw conclusions differently. *You can choose* different actions to apply to feelings and moods, and *practice them*. Over time, those new actions become new habits, which support your change project instead of inhibiting it.

Finally, during a long change project, the most important Thinking and Doing habit changes involve those that boost motivation or get you to take helpful action without requiring as much emotionally "juice." The next chapter describes this phenomenon in detail.

Chapter 3: Let's look at motivation

Everybody wants *to feel like* doing something *before they do it.*
I'm like that, and so are my friends, family, and coaching
clients. The only thing better than feeling like it would be
*really, **really** feeling like it.* Yet, anyone who's ever completed
a long, challenging project knows how important it is to be
productive even on days when you aren't feeling it.

This chapter explores the tension between these two truths:

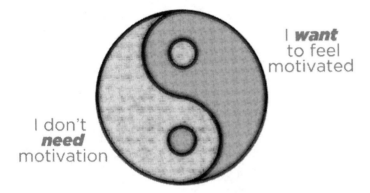

Managing the complex relationship between motivation and
action is important when striving for change in your life.

This chapter discusses:

- *A story about motivation*—Explore motivational break
  downs and breakthroughs in this story about a client
  facing serious challenges during a long-term change
  effort.

- *How does motivation work?*—Understand whether you are positively or negatively motivated, so you can use techniques that work best for you.

- *How focus affects motivation*—Pay attention to details and build focusing skills so you can maintain consistent behavior needed to create new habits.

- *How to use motivation well*—Learn when to boost motivation and when it's beside the point.

- *How to jump start motivation*—Use these tips for getting yourself to act before feeling motivated.

- *How to "slip into a groove" without motivation*—Use these techniques to get in touch with deeper, truer intentions that support your change effort.

- *How fear and depression trump motivation*—Understand how fear interferes with maintaining motivation, and the importance of recognizing and managing moods.

- *Let's sum it up*—Let's review before you move on to read about what influences us to change.

The next section tells the story of a client who struggled mightily to begin taking action, and the breakthrough moment that led to more seriousness effort.

A STORY ABOUT MOTIVATION

Let's begin with a story about fierce resistance to change.

For more than a year, I'd been working with an intriguing client whom we'll call Samantha. Samantha was a very polite, 38-year-old, single, professional woman who had recently broken up with her partner. She described being an intense people pleaser, feeling severely anxious when inactive and sitting still, and using frantic activity in an attempt to "fill the void inside." Also, Sam reported struggling with periodic bouts of binge drinking and compulsive shopping; she attended AA meetings occasionally but had very mixed feelings about
12-Step Programs.

Consider this example of how every-day occurrences could rattle her emotionally: Samantha's boss had recently made a mild, teasing joke about her in a staff meeting, she interpreted it very personally and negatively, and she requested a one-on-one to talk about the comment. Despite regular promotions, an excellent salary, and abundant evidence from her coworkers that she was held in very high esteem, the joking remark rattled and angered her. During the meeting, the boss needed considerable time to talk her down, reassuring Samantha over and over again that she had meant nothing by the joke and that Sam was a highly valued member of the team.

On the positive side, Samantha was a very successful employee for a major company. She made a good living, owned her own home, formed very loyal friendships, and was an avid runner who participated in several marathons a year. She was also a dedicated client, attending our meetings, being unflinchingly honest, and listening well.

In very brief summary and to be as frank as possible, our one year of Life & Career Coaching didn't accomplish much. I coached her to make a number of different habit changes. I also introduced her to mindfulness exercises and techniques for reducing negative thinking and anxiety. Although she understood our conversations, she consistently failed to practice in between sessions. We tried postponing work on the drinking problem, moving it up to the top priority, attending AA, not attending AA, and attending different meetings, yet the sober-binging pattern kept repeating over and over again. We had *numerous* conversations about letting go of control and how important that was to her well-being, but she still tried frantically to get people to approve of and like her.

Although this is true of everyone facing a major change, Samantha was one of the most extreme examples of this dynamic that I had ever encountered:

When I tried helping her to evaluate how things were going wrong, I'd get a slew of "I don't knows." When she failed to complete a goal, I'd ask Samantha what she was thinking and feeling just before not following through on her commitment. She told me that she'd feel resentful and irritable, and that she'd often think, *Why do I have to do this? Nobody **else** has to work this hard? This isn't fair.* After I'd worked with Samantha for a while and gained her trust, she allowed me to give this type of negative thinking a nickname: we laughed and called it her Inner Brat. We used some techniques to get Samantha to talk to her Inner Brat, to negotiate a truce…but that technique also failed to produce results.

As we entered into our second year of work, I began to notice her taking prolonged breaks, expressing interest in seeking services from other professionals, and struggling to schedule appointments. Sensing that she was just not that into it, I prepared myself for an end to our work.

When she came in for her next appointment, before any words were exchanged, *I immediately noticed a significant difference.* First, there was more of a sense of peace and calm than I'd ever remembered observing. I started the session the way I always do and asked her what was up, how had things been going in recent weeks? And then she told me.

While on vacation, Samantha decided to go skydiving.

She said that the thought had scared the heck out of her initially, but she decided to sign up, board the plane, and go through with it anyway. The anxious thoughts persisted as the plane climbed higher and higher. When the time came to approach the doorway to jump, she told me about a split-second decision she made: *just let go*. She didn't use those exact words, but I remember the theme of what she was trying to convey: a sense of *surrendering completely to the moment*, allowing herself to engage and participate minus *any* resistance or reservations.

It was then that she stepped into the sky.

 Samantha had a clear memory of that rush of wind. There was also the amazing vista she witnessed as she descended. Sam also described the exhilaration of what it feels like to be in a free fall. The skydiving instructor strapped to her back would open the parachute when the time came, so for now she could truly let go and just take in the experience as it was unfolding. Samantha said that while she was in the sky, she thought, *Mindfulness! Just focus on enjoying the ride.*

Since the skydiving episode, Samantha had dedicated herself to attending 90 AA meetings in 90 days, and she'd been to one daily since her vacation ended. This wasn't just moving from inaction to action. Indeed, it was taking on the most ambitious, commitment-testing challenge offered in 12-Step programs.

Yet, instead of looking intimidated, she seemed calm...*and happy*.

*   *   *

Let's review a few helpful lessons from this story.

First, notice that the methodical habit-change methods described in the first two chapters didn't work for Samantha during our first year of work. It took an *emotional catalyst*, some event that shook her sense of self, and that challenged her approach, lifestyle, and notions about what was possible. After skydiving, she was motivated to *take action* instead of *just thinking about it*.

As demonstrated by my Belly Reduction Program story, I needed the embarrassment of not fitting into my pants to get back to the gym; she needed the extreme intensity of skydiving to teach her to relax and submit to "the here and now."

Second, the skydiving incident wasn't a magic cure. In a recent session, Samantha and I laughed and talked about her Inner Brat resurfacing, and she still had other personal issues that needed work. As outlined in the previous chapter, old habits linger until new habits overpower them, and it takes committed action *over time* to create new habits.

Now that we've taken a look at a detailed example of someone facing motivational challenges, let's take a look at finer details about how motivation does and doesn't work. The next section discusses a few general patterns of motivational responses.

.HOW DOES MOTIVATION WORK?

OK, you want to get unstuck and create some change in your life. *So, what's your motivation?*

As mentioned in the previous chapter, cues and cravings and rewards pull you back into old habits, and it's going to take a new set of cues and cravings and rewards to solidify your desired change. However, it takes repetition over time before new habits become automatic. Until then, you'll periodically need to remind yourself why you're putting in such effort. To motivate yourself well, it can be helpful to understand how motivation works.

First, understand that you're motivated by a number of different factors, such as basic biology, instinct, incentives, various drives, the urge to reduce arousal to feel calmer, the value you place in self-actualization, and more.[30] Motivation can be *positive* (wanting what you'll gain) or *negative* (avoiding what you'll lose); motivation can come from within you (*intrinsic*) or from outside of you (*external*).[31]

To further understand positive and negative motivation, let's briefly review the *operant conditioning principles* put forth by psychologist B. F. Skinner. As you may recall, a behavior either increases or decreases based on what you get out of it. A behavior can be *strengthened* by gaining something good or getting rid of something bad, both of which can be seen as different types of **rewards**. A behavior can be *weakened* by experiencing something bad or losing something good, which can be seen as different types of **punishments**.[32]

For example, if you do something that gives you more money, compliments from others, pride in yourself, or more social status, then you're likely to do it again; also *if it gets rid of* not having enough money, feeling ashamed for failing, disappointment from loved ones, or lack of social respect, then you're *also* likely to do it again. It depends on how you look at it, right? Getting something good or getting rid of something bad can both motivate you and increase the likelihood that you'll keep behaving that way.

Of course, the opposite is true. If you behave in a way that results in something bad or gets rid of something good, then you're likely to stop the behavior.

As the previous chapter pointed out, old habits never really go away; you either need to change an old habit or create a new, stronger one. So when it comes to resisting old habits and choosing new behavior, it's best to focus on strengthening the new behavior until it becomes rock solid, automatic. To motivate yourself, you can focus on either the positive or negative consequences involved with your change.

Both negative and positive consequences motivate everyone. That being said, people can have a strong tendency one way or the other. It can be helpful if you know whether you're more *positively motivated* or *negatively motivated*. If you're more positively motivated, you want to focus on and emphasize the benefits of change; if you are more negatively motivated, focus on and play up avoiding how unpleasant the situation will be if you don't change.

I'll often ask my clients, *If I said that I'd give you $100 to do a task, or if I said that I'll take $100 out of your bank account for failing to do it, which more strongly makes you want to act?* If you get more excited at the prospect of what you'll gain, that's positive motivation. If avoiding the loss lights the hotter fire under your butt, that's negative motivation.

Neither is better or worse. They both work equally well.

Most people are negatively motivated, but many struggle to understand this because being positively motivated just sounds so much hipper and more desirable. For example, I worked with a client who was procrastinating about a job search. After having a conversation about what motivates her, she swore up and down that she was positively motivated. Then during the next few meetings, I pointed out that all her recent decisions to stop procrastinating were based on avoiding bad consequences: frustration from her husband, feeling disappointed due to not acting sooner, and embarrassment about others possibly finding out about her procrastination. It turned out that she was strongly, *strongly* negatively motivated.

Continuing from the previous example, that client discovered why some of her Self Talk didn't work very well. When she and those around her asked, *Don't you want a job? Don't you want money coming in again? Won't you feel relief getting this done quicker?*, they were unknowingly tempting her with prizes that didn't excite her. The following questions would have worked better: *Wouldn't you hate having to ask your parents for another loan? Wouldn't you like to stop disappointing your husband? Aren't you concerned about your unemployment running out? Wouldn't you feel proud of yourself if you avoided these bad things?*

If you're negatively motivated, be careful not to use language that kicks up guilt and especially shame, because those feelings can result in shutting down instead of feeling motivated. Managing guilt and shame is a big topic that's beyond the scope of *Daily Pivots*. However, here's a tip: judge the (in)action negatively, *not yourself.* As a brief example, focus on how good and proud you'll feel by avoiding the bad consequences; avoid toxic Self Talk that emphasizes that you're a "bad" person who "should" be doing something different. (For exercises that can help with this, see *Appendix B: Let's look at thinking habits.*)

*   *   *

Let's briefly apply some of these motivation principles to the story at the beginning of this chapter.

Samantha appeared to be *positively* and *extrinsically* motivated; none of the negative consequences of the previous year—her partner breaking up with her, embarrassing alcohol binges, disappointment from friends, missing work due to hangovers, shame for having failed—were enough to motivate her to change. It wasn't until she experienced something positive outside of her own internal world of thoughts and feelings—the skydiving experience—that she understood on a deep level the kind of excitement and exhilaration that comes from letting go of fear and "going for it" in life.

*   *   *

Now that we've discussed how motivation works, it calls into question *how it fails*. The next section provides a tip for maintaining motivation during long-term change.

How focus affects motivation

When most of us embark on a project, we're usually brimming with motivation. Yet over time, enthusiasm can wax and wane, come and go. Reflect back on a time during a long project when you were having an off day or when your motivation was low, and then remember the surge of energy you felt as soon as you vividly recalled all the good that was going to come your way once the project was complete.

For example, it's the moment when your mind refocuses from how hard it is denying yourself that cheeseburger to the pride you feel when you run your hand over your tighter stomach. Or it's the moment your mind shifts from the drudgery of completing your 5-mile run today to how it'll feel when you cross the finish line of the New York City Marathon next fall.

Funny how quickly it can come back, right? To make this happen, shift focus from today's task (*your goal*) to the reward you'll get at the end of your change efforts (*your vision of success*).

Of course, it often takes more than a shift of perspective to boost motivation. The following section describes when and how motivation is helpful during a long-term change effort, and provides more detailed tips for boosting motivation.

How to use motivation well

Let's review a graphic used at the beginning of this chapter:

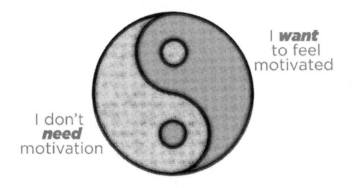

On the one hand when it comes to sustained and intense motivation, you need more of it for a long-term project than you do to satisfy an urge to see a movie or to take a walk. On the other hand, the vast majority of actions you'll undertake during a major project require no emotion; you just need to get yourself to do it.

Let's take a look at how change requires different types of emotional focusing during the project:

1. You need **initial motivation** to start a big project—the vision of success energizes you.

2. You need **commitment** to take daily action—no motivation necessary.

3. You need some **motivational booster shots** throughout the project—strengthen your belief in success periodically as you go.

A catalyst can provide initial motivation to start your project. For example, not fitting into my pants got me to embark on my Belly Reduction Program, and skydiving motivated Samantha to begin curbing her control-freak tendencies.

When it comes to commitment, don't get too heavy or intimidated by that word. Commitment is just an *agreement* or *promise* you make to yourself that you'll act. That's all.

To bring this down to earth, let's look at an extended example. Let's say you'd like to alter what you eat to improve your weight and health. Maybe you spent months or even years denying the need for change, thinking about it, and preparing for it. In a sense, even though there hasn't been a large amount of observable progress, you've been working on building your initial motivation throughout that time.

After thinking and preparing, you finally decide to take action aimed at eating healthier, and your commitment to the project begins. Notice the subtle difference between *feeling* like doing something and *deciding* to do it. If you feel like doing something, there's a tiny bit of wiggle room for you to back out; if you truly *decide* to do something, *it's a done deal*, even though you haven't taken action yet. A firm decision includes deep feelings of willingness and inevitability.

In the beginning, your initial motivation is still front and center, and that energy fuels your commitment. You're willing to try new techniques for buying, cooking, snacking on, and eating your food. There are even times when you push through without needing to feel good about what you're doing. That initial momentum carries you along.

Though as mentioned in the last chapter, willpower is a muscle that can tire when used too much. If you don't rest those muscles, you can become vulnerable to emotional eating, the convenience of the drive-through window, or the lure of a candy dish at work. Sometimes you just feel weary. Sometimes you get distracted.

When feeling this way, you need either to give your willpower a brief rest or give yourself a motivational booster shot. Here are two ways you can boost your motivation periodically as you work on a long-term change project:

- Measure your progress
- Use extended Self Talk to adjust either the original vision or how you feel about it

If it looks as if your change program is working, then your motivation is likely to go up. For example, you can weigh yourself regularly, so that you both chart your progress (which boosts motivation) and notice when you're off track (so you can adjust what you're doing).

Finally, although it's too clumsy for daily use, there are times when you'll need to give yourself a motivational pep talk. To do this, I recommend using either an *Appreciative Inquiry* or

Motivational Interviewing technique, which are conversational methods designed to refocus and boost motivation.

Both motivational techniques are helpful methods for balancing two very important needs when it comes to recommitting to project goals:

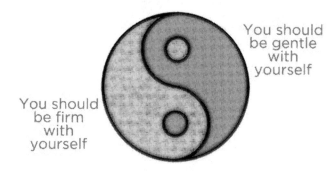

You should be gentle with yourself

You should be firm with yourself

Appreciative Inquiry methods focus on recognizing what's going well, imagining things going even better, deciding what else needs to happen, and picking one manageable task that you'd be willing to do right now that will move your project closer to completion.[33] It's a way to avoid getting bogged down by problems and to focus instead on solutions that build off of past success. For example, if quickly snacking on a protein bar at work is a part of your change project that's going well, then what other nutrition and exercise activities can you imagine that would also fall into the category of "quick and easy"? Of the things you just imagined, what are you *willing* to try first?

To use *Motivational Interviewing*, apply a gentle, collaborative tone of voice as you remind yourself of the original vision for change: *to weigh less and enjoy the benefits of being healthier.* Then without judging, compare the vision to the task you're currently struggling to do: for example, *resisting the urge to pig out on pizza tonight.* [34]

This is a technique for being respectful about the mixed feelings we have about change:

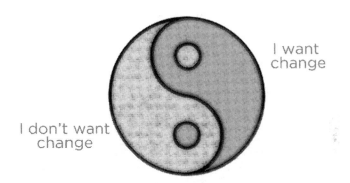

Gently acknowledge that right at this moment you both want it and don't want it, and that it's important to honor both feelings. Ask yourself if the end goal is still important to you. (*Really?*) Explore your objections. Consider your options: for example, take a night off from the project, pause the project indefinitely, cancel it, or revisit the current goal. Be patient and flexible. Let answers reveal themselves to you over time. Be willing to experiment with different approaches as "food for thought."

By slowing down, getting real, and thinking things through, some creative and helpful ideas can emerge. Sometimes, you'll just submit and recommit to doing the task, though you may discover more interesting choices. You may realize that today's goal is too big and needs to be broken into smaller tasks. You might decide to alter your end vision somewhat given lessons learned along the way. You may need to get some help to complete the current task, or maybe you need to back off and do some preparation before returning to the troublesome task.

Getting back to our nutrition and weight-loss example, here are a few simple adjustments that can come from honest Self Talk. A handful of peanuts may work better for you than almonds, even though all the articles say almonds are healthier. You may decide that joining Weight Watchers wasn't for you at the beginning of the project, but group support could really help at this stage of the effort. Or you may decide to scale back that goal you had for total weight loss before the holiday season and aim for next summer instead. Maybe elliptical machines and treadmills don't work for you, and you can better engage your willpower if you use boxing exercises instead.

Whatever you finally decide, the end result is peace of mind, a sense that the next step you're about to take is do-able, and a renewed desire to do what it takes to make it happen. It should result in getting unstuck and flowing again.

You were easy on yourself in that you were patient, willing to negotiate, compassionate, and flexible. At the same time, *you were firm with yourself*, because you never let yourself off the hook easily and quickly; you kept a strong focus on achieving your vision for change.

*　　*　　*

As one final note before closing, I strongly recommend that you limit the number of times you decide to push ahead when you aren't enjoying yourself. Enjoying yourself along the way—as well as feeling in control—conserves willpower and boosts motivation to stick with your program.

As mentioned earlier in this section, sometimes you have to submit, honor your commitment, and *just do it*. Having said that, there are times when we may need some slick methods for convincing ourselves to forge ahead like that. The next section provides a few tips and techniques that can help you in those moments when your commitment is waning, and you don't have the time or inclination for a big, hairy pep talk.

HOW TO JUMP START MOTIVATION

So, you don't need to feel motivation during every moment of your project, and substituting commitment for motivation can help you *just do it*. Nevertheless, it raises this question: *What can I do if I'm in a particularly bad way, and I'm juuust about to get off track and do something I'll regret later?*

Well, I have a technique that can help. To introduce it, let me share a brief story.

Almost twenty years ago, after the break-up of a four-year relationship, my partner and I dissolved our home and divided our belongings, and I moved into an apartment with a roommate. In general, I landed in a very good place. Even so, that didn't eliminate all of the pain and struggle. I felt a bit down.

During this time, I was working a full-time job, earning my master's degree, and doing a 16-hour-a-week unpaid internship. I was often exhausted, overwhelmed, and fearfully avoidant.

Late one weekend afternoon, I was lying in my bed attempting to nap, literally pulling the covers over my head. On that day, I was feeling intimidated by the prospect of getting my checkbook and bills in order, cleaning my office, and decluttering. Part of me wanted to procrastinate by escaping into a long nap, and another part of me felt so bad about myself for running away from something so easy to do.

Instead of falling asleep, a thought occurred to me: *What if I did just a little bit?* Still hiding under the covers, I posed another question to myself, asking if I'd be willing to pay three bills, no more. *Just do three of them, OK?* It was a gentle, reasonable request, and the answer felt very clear: *Yes...OK.*

So, I got up slowly, still not feeling terribly energized, but glad that I was able to get myself out of bed and moving again. I went to the desk, and I began to face what I'd been avoiding.

You know when you get wrapped up in an activity, it takes on a momentum, and it carries you along so you end up doing more than you had intended? That's exactly what happened at the desk. I paid those three bills, and afterward it just felt easy to keep going a little longer. I paid all of the bills for the month and decluttered my desk slightly as I worked.

The entire episode lasted not much longer than an hour. After I was done, I remember still feeling a bit draggy but much better than before, and I was ready to get on with my day. The crippling shame and fear were gone.

In the moment when I could have chosen to continue with dysfunctional nap taking, I had a brief talk with myself, and decided to pivot into a new direction and do something different. Over the course of my adult life, exactly what I've said to myself has varied, but the purpose of the Self Talk remains the same: *what can I say to convince myself to avoid the bad habit and pivot into what I really want to do?* My Self-Talk conversation shifts me out of automatic behavior and into *choice*.

*   *   *

Let's take my personal story, and let's extract a tactic you can use when commitment is seriously lacking and you don't feel like doing what you need to do:

Resisting doing something?

Ask yourself to do the task for ONLY 30 minutes.

At the end of 30 minutes, if you're hating, *hating*, HATING it, then you have permission to stop. Just do it for a little while, and see how you feel at the end of the half hour.

Remember that at one time, you were motivated to begin your personal project. It's just that you've temporarily lost focus and commitment. You need a reminder as to why you wanted to do the project in the first place, and taking a small amount of action is often all it takes to refresh your motivational memory.

Once you get moving, you'll find that it actually feels pretty good, and you'll often continue past the 30-minute mark. Once in a blue moon, you'll decide to stop the activity after a half hour. Maybe you're feeling under the weather physically, or some other priority is demanding that you shorten the activity. Though most of the time, *motivation will follow the action.* Act on commitment, and positive feelings for the project reemerge after you get going.

This technique is very similar to another one that's very popular with my clients. A renowned psychiatrist named Edward M. Hallowell, M.D., Ed.D., wrote a book entitled *Worry*, which contains a very helpful approach to anything weighing on your mind.

His technique is called Evaluate, Plan, and Remediate (EPR),[35] I'll present my modified two-step version of this approach:

1. Ask yourself if there's anything that you can do now—today, this week—to address whatever's causing your worry.

2. *If yes*, then do it as soon as possible, and scratch it off the list.

    If no, then remind yourself that *you have done everything that you can for now*, ask for trust that you'll take care of business once you can do more, and *accept the current situation as is.*

Of course, taking a small action is easier than accepting that there's nothing more that can be done. Still and all, people usually relax somewhat if they know in their heart of hearts that they've done everything possible for now. Finally, notice how my story about getting out of bed and paying a few bills fits nicely into Hallowell's model; instead of feeling crushed by dozens of things that I couldn't possibly accomplish in one afternoon, I felt better once I focused on one small, simple task, leaving the rest for another day.

*   *   *

On the one hand, you can use a significant amount of structure, focus, and effort to maintain both commitment and motivation. On the other hand, if there's an easier way to get motivated, it would be worth considering, right? The next section provides you with a quicker, leap-of-faith way to feel better about returning to your change project.

HOW TO "SLIP INTO A GROOVE" WITHOUT MOTIVATION

To get a feel for motivation-boosting and focusing tactics, let's quickly review a list:

> *Theeere's*...positive reinforcement, negative reinforcement, internal motivation, external motivation, shifting your focus, calendaring, To Do lists, reminder notes, mentoring or counseling support, group support, slowing down, meditating, measuring your progress,

Appreciative Inquiry, Motivational Interviewing, the 30-minute technique, and the Hallowell technique.

Phew, that's a lot! Although you don't have to use every technique every time, building structure and habits designed to keep you motivated and focused can seem overwhelming.

Sometimes, I think it's a choice between putting forth serious effort or *learning how to get out of your own way.* Getting out of your own way isn't an instant fix; it *does* require that you work on forming a few new habits. That being said, if you can dedicate yourself to this approach, you'll be able to motivate yourself and get back on track quicker and easier than creating an elaborate set of routines designed to keep yourself in line.

To understand how to do this, it's vital that you be clear about the subtle-but-important differences between these two emotional states:

- *Feeling* like doing something

- *Intending* to do something

Feelings are fleeting; they are the breezes that blow over the surface of the earth, bending the plants and tree branches of our daily actions. To illustrate how emotions are designed to be very temporary states, consider this scenario: you walk down the street, and you see a funny billboard and laugh. A car then drives too closely to you, hits a puddle, and splashes dirty water on your pants; you feel angry. After brushing off, you continue walking, and you spot a couple arm-in-arm and clearly in love. Your heart warms and softens, and you smile as you walk past them. Moment to moment, the gust of your current emotion blows you in a potentially different direction.

(Feelings can linger over time to form powerful *moods*, which are more like storm-force winds. Managing moods is beyond the scope of *Daily Pivots*. However, to learn research-backed methods for managing difficult moods, see *Appendix A: Let's look at mindfulness* and *Appendix B: Let's look at thinking habits*.)

In contrast, *intentions* are often linked to a much larger purpose or goal; they are the strong, underground river that nourishes the plants and trees of our actions. It's the solid feeling that occurs when you're in touch with your vision for change, decision to do it, motivation to keep moving, confidence in a plan, commitment to executing it, and the need to make it happen *all at the same time*. When all of that is clear and in focus, you *intend* to make it so.

Using a weight-loss example, my *tasks* for the day are to exercise and eat well. My *purpose* is to lose weight, look good, and feel healthy. My *intention* is to be a focused, healthy person who loves myself. A focused, healthy person who loves himself *can't help* but to exercise and eat right; it springs naturally from the kind of person he intends to be.

To increase the likelihood of follow-through and success, take action while at the same time keeping a gentle focus on your underlying intention. The *Daily Pivots* method, as described in Part II of this book, includes tips for recognizing and honoring your intentions. Also, although there are a number of excellent resources that you can choose to explore the concept of intention, I recommend *Mallika Chopra's panel discussion on YouTube entitled Mindfulness & Intention*[36] (http://tinyurl.com/mindfulness-intention).

In my work with Life & Career Coaching clients, I've encountered a deeper, more difficult kind of emotional shut down that happens when there is a very specific conflict of intention. When your intention to be your best self (by working on your change project) conflicts with your hardwired, in-born intention to protect yourself from harm, then the unfortunately frequent result is that goal achievement stalls, people feel distressed in a number of ways, and self-esteem can take a hit.

Let me share a recent example from my client work. One person who had been using a failing job-search strategy for a few years during the depths of the Great Recession was very hesitant to submit her vastly improved resume. She explained that, after years of submitting resumes and getting almost no interviews, she couldn't bear any more failure. In her mind, if she submitted a resume and didn't get an interview, then that would be an Epic Fail. So, she avoided it. To make progress, we worked to redefine success from "getting an interview" to "submitting five resumes a week." Until we removed the threat of failure, she was stuck and unable to move forward.

Nobody is interested in sticking a hand into an emotional meat grinder. If you're facing this type of conflicted intention, refocus on your change project until it shifts from feeling threatening to challenging-but-do-able. Once the project is no longer *threatening*, you won't face the intense need to *protect* yourself from it.

Thankfully, your intention to build the life you've dreamed of having is deeper and stronger than any fleeting emotion, and it's even mightier than some fear that says you need to defend yourself from some vague boogeyman. Nonetheless, you'll need a few tactics you can use to refocus on your deeper intention in moments of weakness.

*   *   *

To get out of your own way, the overall goal is to be clear about your deepest, most positive intentions and your desire to act in a way that honors them. Several of the steps in the list that follows are part of any mindfulness practice; however, I highlight them here as a way for you to get started quickly.

When you're feeling a strong emotional pull away from your change project:

1. Stop whatever you're currently doing, and exit the room as a way to take a *mini-break*. In addition, you can walk outdoors or walk up to a window to give yourself more of a view.

   Whenever feeling strong emotions, *speed is your enemy*. It always helps to take a break, to slow down.

2. Take a few deep breaths and concentrate on how the air feels moving past your nostrils and filling your

chest, and follow the sensations of your breath in and out.

3. Clear your mind of thoughts other than your breathing and sensations in your body.

4. Scan your body for any tension and tightness, and try to tighten and then relax your muscles, stretching and loosening them.

5. After 10 to 15 seconds of relaxing, ask yourself: *OK. What's my intention, here?*

6. Continue to stretch and relax and breathe, keep your mind clear, and *wait for the answer to occur to you.* You may just sense the answer, or it may pop into your mind as a thought or image.

7. Make a decision about what you're going to do as a way of acting out of your intention.

8. Do it immediately.

When you ask, *What is my intention, here?*, you're asking yourself to honor who you are at your core, at your best. It's a request that you honor your agreement—*a promise*—to follow through with your change project. *How do you want to be about this? What do you want to do right now so that, after you're finished, you'll feel proud of how you responded and not feel disappointed in yourself?*

I've used this "what is my intention?" technique recently, and it worked very well. I found that just asking about my intention wakes me from a kind of anxious trance, reminds me that my choice is connected to something much bigger and deeper, and makes taking different action easier. It feels like slipping back into a groove, or letting the river of intention pull your canoe along without you having to paddle so hard.

When it comes to a conflict between change and a need to protect yourself, it may take some additional Self Talk to choose your change project. When facing that conflict, select a Pivot Inspiration in *PART II: JUST GET TO THE POINT ALREADY!* that addresses and calms your fear. When you reduce fear in that way, your deeper intention becomes clearer and more compelling.

We've just covered a technique for addressing and moving past fear. Even so, it can be helpful to explore further the effect fear can have on your change project. Even small amounts of fear can impair and reduce your ability to make good decisions and take effective action. The next section discusses this issue in more detail.

How fear and depression trump motivation

When we resist helpful, desirable change, there's almost always some type of fear lurking below our awareness. When afraid—*even just slightly afraid*—it's really difficult to focus on anything other than feeling relief, which is a goal that kicks to the curb any plan to honor personal growth.

It isn't so much that fear destroys motivation; it's that fear hijacks the entire change process, and motivates you to seek out safety and soothing instead. You actually become *very highly motivated* to end the threat so that you can feel safe again. Also, fear can wildly distort reality, reducing your ability to perceive what's going on around you, to act creatively, and to use resources to solve problems.

Any amount of fear, anxiety, or stress is significantly debilitating.

To get a sense of the seriousness of fear-based debilitation, I recommend that you watch *a brief YouTube video from Simons and Chabris (1999)*[37] (http://tinyurl.com/fear-limits-you). The effect of this video can be much more powerful when watched on a very large screen; I saw it among an audience of 100 people at a mind-body seminar. 60% of the people said that they were initially unaware of "it" but saw it after a while, and I was part of the 40% *who never saw it.* Watch the video, and you'll understand what I mean.

Here's its main point: a little bit of performance anxiety applied to a meaningless task can cause your brain to filter out parts of reality (literally erasing something from this video), which makes it extremely-difficult-to-impossible for you to perceive what is right in front of you, let alone make good decisions.

Let me share an example as to why it's actually very helpful that our brains have this capability to filter and hyper-focus. Imagine that you're hiking, you take a few steps off the path, and you notice that you're near a ledge. Let's say that you look over the ledge and see a huge drop into a ravine...*you're on the edge of a cliff*. Feeling threatened by the potential fall triggers your *fight-or-flight-or-freeze response*. This response is helpful in that it hyper-focuses you on the threat, allowing you to stop moving forward and to concentrate on stepping back until safe again.

While your bodily systems are working at full capacity to get you to safety, there are many things you aren't noticing, because they have nothing to do with reducing the threat. For example, your brain is filtering out the clouds, the beautiful blue sky, the eagle flying nearby, and the types of trees on either side of you as you're backing away from the cliff.

When facing a life-threatening emergency, this level of hyper-focus is efficient and very helpful. Your focus can broaden once you're safe again.

However, for modern life's more complicated and subtle challenges, hyper-focus can be a problem. For example, we can overreact to a boss, a father-in-law, a traffic jam, minor weight gain, or getting a speeding ticket in the same way that we react to a rattlesnake, a mugger's knife, or nearly falling off a cliff. *Fear makes us overreact to non-life-threatening situations.*
In addition to fear, people can also struggle with depression. One of the key symptoms of depression is *hopelessness*, which we can define as a fearful belief that things won't work out or that a bad situation will never get any better. Learning skills to lessen symptoms of diagnosable anxiety and depressive disorders is beyond the scope of *Daily Pivots*; please consult a medical practitioner to see if medical treatment is recommended for feelings of anxiety or depression.

If you find that fear is the main reason you get stuck while working on change, I strongly recommend developing a meditative practice, which will help you to stay anchored more peacefully in the present moment and to stay focused on what you can actually accomplish in the "here and now." For brief tips about developing a mindfulness practice, see *Appendix A: Let's look at mindfulness.*

Here are some fear-reduction tips that can assist you with staying motivated:

- Overwhelm can generate anxiety, and the 30-minute technique described in the *How to jump start motivation* section is designed to help you refocus on a manageable task.

- If you feel overwhelmed by everything on your project's To-Do list, then consider backing off of action for a while. Perhaps you need to do some preparation before your To-Do list items feel more manageable. Maybe you need some Appreciative Inquiry or Motivational Interviewing Self Talk to refresh your desire for the end goal. Doing work before you're ready to do it is anxiety provoking; back up and refocus on research and decision-making.

- If you're keeping a very large and overwhelming To-Do list in your head, then try reducing it to items that need to be done today and then one big item for "everything else you need to do in the future." In this way, the number of items on your To-Do list can drop from, say, 32 items to 5, with one being "everything I need to do starting tomorrow." Once things calm down, you can create individual To-Do items further into the future.

Also, getting your To-Do list out of your head and onto paper or into your electronic device can calm you.

- The deadliest words for someone experiencing anxiety are the words "what if?" On the one hand, human beings are wonderfully creative creatures. On the other hand, we have an endless ability to conjure scary future scenarios, and it's impossible to prove whether they will or won't happen. The solution is to avoid thinking in "what ifs" and refocus on "just today." When things are very, very stressful in my clients' lives, I recommend chunking the day into even smaller segments: for example, instead of focusing on "one day at a time," focus on "one hour at a time."

- Exposure treatment is a research-backed method of reducing anxiety disorders, and I highly recommend it for dealing with irrational fears that stand between you and your goals. This technique is beyond the scope of this book; consult with an experienced, licensed mental health counselor for more information about exposure treatment.

For Pivot Inspirations designed to help you pivot away from fear reactions and into a calmer state, try using the stories in the *Calming anxiety and fear*, *Focusing*, *Letting go of control*, and *Relaxing about mistakes* chapters in Part II. For brief tips about altering thinking patterns as a way to avoid stress, depression, and anxiety, see *Appendix B: Let's look at thinking habits.*

The next section reviews topics discussed in this chapter and gives you some food-for-thought before moving on to the next chapter.

Let's sum it up

Motivation is a slippery beast. Everybody wants it, no one can have it all the time, and different techniques work for different situations.

As discussed in this chapter, you can often use willpower and commitment to push yourself through day-to-day activities without motivation. Yet given that willpower weakens over time unless it gets some rest, that's not a workable long-term strategy.

In order to apply motivation to any long-term change project, I think you have to learn how to work it, ignore it, and transcend it, choosing an approach in the moment that's most needed. Let me share two scenes from TV shows that demonstrate this point.

I was watching the TV show *The Amazing Race* recently, and each pair of contestants had to guide a narrow, canoe-shaped boat through a series of shallow canals. One team member stood at the front, and the other stood at the back and guided the boat using a long pole to push off the bottom of the canal. At the beginning of the course, the water current moved in the same direction as the boat, so it was easy for the team member in the back to steer. Yet when exiting one canal and moving into another, they found themselves going *against the new current* instead of flowing with it.

Teams that quickly shifted the pilot from the back of the boat to the front fared well. The two teams that failed to make that adjustment and continued to pilot from the back were pulled way off course. The failing teams didn't have a motivational problem; instead, they needed a more efficient strategy than "do the same thing, only harder." Get out of your head, get out of your own way, and figure out what needs to be done moment to moment

Also recently, I was watching an episode of the TV show *The Biggest Loser*. The trainer, Bob Harper, instructed two contestants to work on a variety of exercises: lifting weights, wiggling heavy ropes, using the exercise bike, and more.
In the middle of the exercises, Bob challenged the contestants by saying, *Finish this sentence for me: **I am**....* As they exercised, contestants shouted out answers, and Bob wrote them on a whiteboard:

I am a warrior

I am strong

I am a champion

I am invincible

I am young (spoken by someone in his 50s)

In this moment, Bob wasn't focusing his clients on the specifics of lifting a dumbbell or running across the gym. He was trying to get them to bring forth their intentions about the kind of person they wanted to be, to get them in touch with who they are at their emotional core. Manifest your intention for who you are in your heart of hearts, bring her or him into the present moment, and that person—*THAT person*—will automatically feel motivated to lift a dumbbell or run across the gym. *That person* will do it without applying motivational techniques or long Self-Talk speeches. *That person* will do it, because those actions flow naturally from a warrior, a strong person, a champion, an invincible person, and a young person.

Of course, it's not magic. Muttering the words won't instantly produce results. You're not a champion or a warrior because you say you are. You're on the road to becoming a champion or a warrior *when you intend to be one*, and when you act out of that intention with consistency and commitment.

To tap into your intention, you have to slow down, quiet your mind, focus on that *deep river of knowing* that runs through all of us, and commit to taking action, whether it be big, medium, or small. Do what you can do today (sometimes that means taking a well-timed rest), and intend to pick it up again tomorrow.

Repeat often, and acting from a place of intention will become your new, automatic habit. Watch that person emerge over time, and *become who you truly are.*

The previous three chapters focused on what individuals can do to set goals, form helpful habits, and manage motivation. As powerful as individual work can be, we are not operating in a vacuum; human beings are social creatures. The next chapter provides some background about how human beings change, and about the social influences that can support or hinder any large change project.

Chapter 4: Let's look at change

Daily Pivots makes frequent mention of *change projects*. Here are some examples presented in previous chapters: my Zen Driving Program, working with a financial planner, the Belly Reduction Program, and Samantha's efforts to ease her anxiety and take more action.

In all of these projects, people moved through predictable stages of change, were inspired by influential people, made adjustments over time, and used conversations with others as a way to generate ideas and stay accountable.

When we embark on any major change project, our efforts will be nudged, assisted, bullied, and guided by how human beings change and by the environment that surrounds us. To succeed, it's helpful to understand the larger context in which you'll be operating.

This chapter discusses:

- *A story about change*—Compare the very different results obtained by two of my clients who used networking to increase job opportunities.

- *The TTM stages of change*—Be prepared for the different needs and impulses you'll feel at various times during your change project.

- *The role of structure*—Understand the need for structured reminders.

- *The role of conversations*—Improve upon the basic information you can get from book research, Internet searches, and taking classes.

- *The role of social environment*—Learn to leverage helpful group influence and resist unhelpful peer pressure.

- *The role of trial and error*—Incorporate and peacefully accept experimentation, learning, and adjusting as normal and important parts of the change process.

- *The role of habits*—Review why habits are the foundation for any change effort.

- *Let's sum it up*—Let's review before you move on to read about Pivot Points.

The next section tells a story about two clients who followed very different paths as they pursued the same type of goal.

A STORY ABOUT CHANGE

I strongly emphasize *informational interviewing* (also called *exploratory interviewing*) with my Career Coaching clients. In very brief summary, an informational interview is a business-casual meeting designed to research a career, an organization, or specific professional opportunities.

When convincing people to try this type of networking, I tell them two client stories representing two polar-opposite results. A client whom we'll call Janet represented 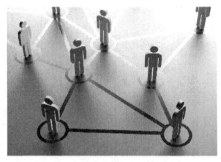 the *long-hard-work* end of the continuum, and a client whom we'll call Adam represented the *quick-and-lucky* end.

Let's start with long-hard-work. In very brief summary, Janet was a 54-year-old married woman with several children enrolled in a private middle school. In addition to being very concerned about age discrimination, Janet worried that her quirky resume and professional background would hold her back. She had recently been doing financial work but had no formal credentials, and she had outdated scientific skills.

Very early in her efforts, Janet decided it was best to work very hard at networking. She prepared by setting up a few easy informational interviews with friendly family members and colleagues, and then she *went nuts with it.*

Janet conducted between 150 and 200 informational interviews in six months. I remember early in her networking project, she unfurled a printed copy of the spreadsheet she used to organize herself. The thing looked like an airplane control panel. There were columns for this and columns for that, notations about how many meetings she'd had with each person, who knew whom, where each person worked, and more. It was *quite impressive*.

So after six months of intense effort, Janet interviewed for and got a *wonderful* position with a venture capital outfit, evaluating medical and scientific companies for possible investment. This is my favorite part of her story: when she did her initial group interview with five people, she had already had "coffee dates" with two of them. Imagine walking into a formal job interview and already knowing two members of the panel!

Now, let's shift gears and take a look at Adam's story. Adam was a 48-year-old single man who recently had been laid off from his position as an office manager for a group of technicians. He was responsible for inventory, hiring, performance management, ensuring proper maintenance of repair vans, and tracking technicians using GPS.

As Adam decompressed during the late fall, I assisted him with putting together his resume and with developing a job-search strategy. Although I emphasized taking his time to find a compatible position, Adam quickly grew nervous about finances just after the New Year, and he grabbed at the first available opportunity. He took a position with a medical-device company, doing basic financial bookwork in a small office inside a warehouse. At that point, we shook hands, and he took a break from our coaching work.

A year later, Adam returned to me for more guidance. He told me that his company had been bought out recently and that he was concerned he'd be laid off. So, we once again updated his resume and reviewed job-searching strategies. Sure enough, before the end of that month, he was let go.

A few months later, Adam began one of our meetings by saying, *I hate to admit this, but you were **right!*** I replied, *What?! What was I right about?*

He then told me that a year-and-a-half earlier, when we first met, I said to him that he knew how to manage an office of technicians and that there must be dozens of such offices nearby. I told him then that he should contact these outfits, say that he's an experienced manager in their line of work, and ask if they could spare 20 minutes to discuss possible opportunities over a cup of coffee.

Finally, Adam was ready to test my advice. He had recently sent one—*ONE!*—email to a former competitor. The competitor replied, *Hey, you used to work for a larger company, and we've just recently begun plans for expanding our operation. You might be able to help us. Come in, and let's talk.*

In very short time, they created a position for Adam and hired him. Note that this opportunity never appeared in any published job ads.

*　*　*

On the one hand, if you look just at the number of networking meetings, then it's clear that Janet put in much more networking time and effort than Adam. In spite of that, when you look at total elapsed time, it took Adam *more than twice as long* to find a great fitting job.

One way to make sense of what happened is to understand that people need to go through a set of stages when they consider taking on a new challenge. For example, people need to understand the need for a change, they need to think about it for a while, they may need to do some preparation, and then they need to take action. Some people take longer in a given stage than others.

As another example, Janet needed only a few conversations with me, and several with her family and close friends, to think it through and prepare for starting a serious networking project. She moved through those stages *in a matter of weeks.* Adam didn't see the need for informational interviews for a *more than a year.* It took working a mediocre job and suffering through another layoff before he realized that he needed to change his approach.

This rest of this chapter discusses various human and social conditions that can affect your long-term change project, and the next section presents information about predictable paths that most of us follow when we seek and initiate major change.

THE TTM STAGES OF CHANGE

Sometimes it doesn't matter in what order you do things. Other times when you do things out of order, you make a big mess. Try baking a cake without first researching the ingredients, or take it out of the oven way too soon. *Yuck.*

Well, it turns out that we human beings tend to make significant life changes in a predictable, orderly process. [38] For example, in my work as a Life & Career Coach, clients can be overly eager to rush into action, and I often find myself coaching them to slow down, do their research, test their theories, and otherwise engage in more preparation before launching into action. The tasks you complete while *considering* a change would be different than the ones you'd do while actively *preparing*; what you do while preparing is very different than your approach as you're *maintaining* an existing change. Taking actions that best support your current state of change leads to feeling calmer, more motivated, focused, and confident.

When beginning work with clients, I like to start by clarifying their current location in the Prochaska-DiClemente model. The formal name for the overall change theory is the *Transtheoretical Model of Behavior Change* or *TTM*.

At the heart of TTM are the *stages of change*. When you look at a change effort from beginning to end, a person typically moves through all stages. However, someone can bounce back and forth, or return to earlier stages, before all is said and done and the change is complete.

Let's take a look at a brief description of each stage:

- **Precontemplation**—The person is unaware of any need to change. I often refer to this as the *Problem? What problem?* stage of change.

- **Contemplation**—Someone is ambivalent, wondering if change is necessary.

- **Preparation**—A person knows that change is needed but wants to get ready first.

- **Action**—The person is ready to begin changing.

- **Maintenance**—She or he is willing to fine tune the change effort over time.

- **Relapse**—The person fell back into an old habit, and can re-enter the change process at any other state.

So in the story presented in the last section, Adam was in the Precontemplation stage for almost a year-and-a-half, not really seeing the need for informational interviewing. Instead, he focused on tuning up his resume, responding to job ads, and making no effort to network.

Janet, on the other hand, moved through Precontemplation, Contemplation, and Preparation in a matter of weeks. The use of that amazingly detailed spreadsheet to track contacts is an example of someone fine-tuning the effort during the Maintenance phase.

When assisting someone in the Precontemplation stage, it's best to provide information very gently as "food for thought." For example, when working with clients in this stage, I find it effective to ask, *What would have to happen to convince you that change might be necessary?* If I had pursued that line of questioning with Adam, he might have answered, *Well, if I don't get any interviews after 3 months of submitting resumes, then maybe I'll need to turn to networking.* Then, back off and let life's circumstances drive whether the person becomes more motivated to change.

When a client is in Contemplation, I'll often suggest a weighted list of Pros and Cons, which clarifies both the advantages and disadvantages of making the change. The term *weighted* means that you assign a number to each item in the list indicating its importance. (*On a scale of 1 to 10, where 1 is "meh, whatever" and 10 is vitally important to you, how important is this item?*) Add the numbers in both columns to compare the total "weight" of the Pros versus the Cons.

If someone needs to get prepared, what specific actions would that person need to complete before beginning the change? If someone is ready to take action, which do-able actions would a beginner be willing to do versus someone who's been working on this change for a while? How can you pace the activities so they don't become overwhelming?

Finally, it's one thing to get a change up and running, but and it's another thing to tune it up over time so it runs more efficiently.

When I was first introduced to this change model, Relapse was not a formal stage. I was very pleased to see its inclusion in recent years. In both my personal and professional experience, it's very helpful to acknowledge that *briefly getting off track and then adjusting* is part of the process of *staying on track.*

For most change efforts, a relapse into an unhelpful habit isn't usually a big deal. Pick yourself up, dust yourself off, and get back on track when you can. For other situations, relapsing can be dangerous, with the most obvious example being attempts to get clean from substances such as heroin. In those cases, it's important to be clear that a relapse can kill.

As examples of relapse, times of intense stress can cause me to drive impatiently or to eat poorly, indicating that I'm off track with my Zen Driving and Belly Reduction programs. When that happens, I consciously focus on stress-reduction techniques, remind myself of strategies that worked well in the past, and recommit to my Action and Maintenance activities until they return to being automatic.

Here are a few points to consider about the TTM stages of change:

- Action isn't the first step; it's not even *close* to being the first step. So, don't judge yourself harshly for not springing immediately into your new, desired change.

- Notice the role that *thinking* plays in the process. Precontemplation requires that you become aware. Contemplation is simply another word for thinking.

Thoughtful planning is helpful for Preparation, Action, and Maintenance.

- Notice the role that *emotion* plays. One of the primary reasons why people linger in the Precontemplation stage is because of potential pain, frustration, or overwhelm they imagine they might feel due to the change; also, some may be in this stage because of comforting older habits. In the Contemplation stage, people are emotionally torn between wanting and not wanting to change:

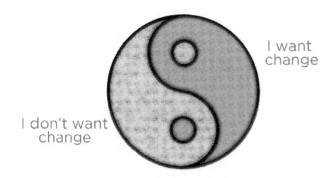

I want change

I don't want change

- This model places a heavy emphasis on problem solving. The previous chapter briefly introduced an approach called the Appreciative Inquiry model, which is a way of focusing on desired change instead of feared problems. Using Appreciative Inquiry, it's possible to skip the Precontemplation and Contemplation stages almost altogether, quickly getting a person into a more willing state to plan and take action.

- I often tell my clients that they need to "make friends" with their mistakes, because errors provide *invaluable information* about how to succeed on the next try. The same can be said of relapses. When it comes to modifying unhelpful habits, relapses provide great information about the cue and reward that drive the unhelpful routine. For example, if loneliness is a cue that triggers emotional eating (which then provides soothing), what else could you do (a new routine) to ease your loneliness?

- Notice the tension between taking care of business today in your current stage of change, while at the same time staying aware of the much larger end goal:

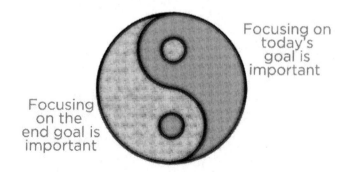

The next section provides very easy and practical ways that structure can assist change.

THE ROLE OF STRUCTURE

As described in *Chapter 2: Let's look at habits*, a habitual behavior starts when you encounter a cue. So, bedtime might cue brushing your teeth, or lunch time on Mondays might cue going to the gym. The cue occurs, and you begin to take action automatically.

Until your new behaviors become more habitual, you need to cue yourself more *explicitly*, which is just a fancy way of saying that you need to find ways to remember to act. Here are some examples of structure that can help jog your memory:

- Write down *compelling reasons* for making a change. Remember to choose positive wording (what you'll gain if you do it) or negative wording (what you'll lose if you don't do it) depending on your natural style of motivation. Here are some methods for recording this information:

  - Index cards

  - Post-its

  - Calendar reminders

  - Smart-phone recordings

  - Notebooks

  - Journals and private blogs

  - Pictures that symbolize your motivation— some people are more visual

Smaller notes on index cards and post-its are good for simple memory jogs, such as "Go running!" or "Snack on an apple." However, smaller notes can boost motivation too; for example, "You'll be sexy in skinny jeans" or "Popping buttons in public—embarrassing!"

Writing in a notebook or private blog is more narrative and conversational. This technique can be particularly helpful for people who are preparing for change but aren't ready yet to make a commitment. Think it through by writing about it.

- Place reminders where you're likely to see them daily:

  - Refrigerator

  - Dashboard of your car

  - Locker at school

  - Online calendar

  - Smart phone or tablet app

  - Bathroom mirror

  - Desk at work

  - Wallet (someplace visible)

- Pick a consistent time when you'll consciously check your reminders. For example, every day at breakfast, flip through your calendar for the day; before going home from work, check your calendar to make sure you know what's happening first thing tomorrow morning. Apps allow you to schedule automated notifications that contact you using your phone or tablet.

- Set up structured meetings and conversations that will hold you accountable and that remind you to take action; for example, you can enlist the help of these professionals:

    - Counselors

    - Coaches

    - Self-help programs

    - Self-improvement programs

    - Support groups

    - A group of friends all working on the same type of goals

I'm reminded of a recent experience with a Life & Career Coaching client. She walked into my office ten minutes late for her appointment, and she said in a harried voice, *Am I supposed to be here today? Is this the right time?* I reassured her that she was in the right place at the right time, and we conducted our meeting.

While setting up another appointment after the meeting, I reminded her, *Be sure to put this in your calendar.* She replied, *Oh, I had today's appointment in my calendar.*

Really?

For this client, the issue wasn't so much that she didn't have enough reminders or structure. Instead, she was allowing everything in her life to proceed too rapidly and impulsively. She had recorded the appointment but didn't have a process noticing her reminder. Setting aside time to slow down and to check the structure already in place would greatly help her change efforts.

The next section provides more detail about how you can conduct different types of conversations that will assist your long-term change projects.

THE ROLE OF CONVERSATIONS

On the one hand, individuals are completely capable of understanding a situation on their own through research, investigation, and trial and error. On the other hand, human beings often use *conversations*—sometimes many, many conversations over a long period of time—to come to an understanding about a complex situation or to make a difficult decision.

Sometimes people engage in *Self Talk*, which is simply a conversation they have with themselves during normal thinking. Notice how Self-Talk conversations can debate, fight, judge, or contradict each other; they can also soothe and provide pep talks.

Sometimes I'll be thinking in one direction about a topic. Moments, hours, or days later, I'll be thinking in a completely different direction. It can take some "back and forth" before my mind finally feels settled.

Let's shift gears and talk about *conversations with others*. If you're struggling to understand something or to make a decision, to whom might you turn for counsel? I suppose the short answer would be *someone you trust*. People who fall into that category might be a spouse, parent, best friend, spiritual adviser, teacher, or trusted counselor.

One factor that could build your trust is whether another person is knowledgeable, experienced, or successful. For example, if you'd like to know what it's like to take a vacation to Disney World, you can have conversations with people who've been there, done that. If you want information about building a model airplane, then ask someone who builds them. Better yet, ask the person who won the model-airplane-building contest last year.

Now, imagine that you've gotten some advice from one person about how to build model airplanes. Then, imagine that you've gotten very different guidance from someone else. What then? Well, they might both be wrong, they might both be right, or the truth may lay somewhere in the middle. There are a number of factors to consider: for example, does one person have more expertise than the other? Does one adviser understand your individual situation, needs, and temperament better?

There's additional action you can take to figure out whose advice to follow. You can do more research, and good research would involve having even *more* conversations. First, you can ask others to help you make sense of conflicting advice. Also, within a larger set of conversations, you can better see trends and patterns. A conversation with three people might yield two or three different opinions; however, "eight out of 10 suggested the same thing" builds confidence in the more popular opinion.

Finally, there are some types of structured conversations in our society that serve very specific purposes. For example, formal classroom teaching establishes a set of roles and expectations that enhance the ability of a teacher to convey information to students. Debates are structured conversations. A Request for a Proposal (RFP) is another example. A jury trial designed to provide a verdict—a rendered decision—is yet another type of structured conversation.

Here are some things to consider about the role of conversations in the change process:

- Notice how structured conversations often serve the purpose of *completing some work*. So, you could think of conversations as assisting the work of adjusting old habits or creating new ones.

- "Deciding to make a change" is a reasonable topic for Self Talk. Sometimes, you tell yourself the decision is firm, you mean it, and you follow through. Sometimes, you tell yourself that the decision is firm, you think that's true, but your follow-through is poor or even non-existent. In the latter case, it's helpful to conduct more Self Talk to tease out the mixed feelings you have about the change.

- You may or may not be consciously aware of your decision to take new action. There are many times in life when we temporarily feel torn between two choices, we may hem and haw briefly, and then we just choose based on a hunch more than on a logical decision (*oh, what the heck?*). That would be an example of the change conversation happening rapidly in your subconscious. There is a growing acknowledgment in the self-help and business arenas that these *intuitive decisions* can sometimes be superior to the more structured, belabored decisions.

Having a conversation with successful people who've done what you want to do can be very useful—more useful than researching it on the Internet or attending a lecture about the topic. Sometimes however, the Internet or lecture can guide you better than the experience of one quirky or lucky individual. Consider this:

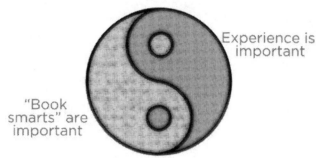

When you have conversations with people, they may disagree with you, sometimes very strongly so. In addition, we are constantly bombarded with different types of messages, such as advertising, conventional wisdom, "common sense," and more. The next section discusses the effect that such messages can have when attempting a long-term change project and what you can do to manage these mixed messages.

THE ROLE OF SOCIAL ENVIRONMENT

Your social environment has a very strong effect on your feelings and on decisions you make. Sometimes, your social environment will have feedback that you'll want to heed. Other times, it will be important to stay firm in your convictions regardless of what others say.

Consider this:

Being true to
yourself is
important

Playing
nicely with
others is
important

When helping people with career changes and job searches, I love to point to them to *an interview with Dr. Jim Bright on YouTube* (http://tinyurl.com/jim-bright). In this video, Dr. Bright presents his *Chaos Theory of Careers*. This video helps frame the topic in a way that gets my clients to relax and that supports having lots of conversations about professions, organizations, and potential career paths.[39]

My favorite line in the video is, *Five-year plan? I don't know what I'm going to be saying **five sentences** from now.* Dr. Bright suggests instead that it would be more helpful for career counselors to broaden the list of considerations when evaluating career options. For example, he said that, if someone feels strongly that she wants to continue in the family business, why should we automatically discourage her based on skill set alone?

When I provide career assistance to my clients, I frequently encounter valid yet non-career reasons for making professional decisions. One example would be *I want to be able to contribute to my daughters' college educations.* My clients often consider travel requirements, flex time or the ability to work from home, not being able to work for others (authority issues), or religious beliefs when making career decisions.

Of course, yielding to your family, friends, or society is not the whole story. Sometimes, it's important to stand your ground no matter what other people think. In my work, I see this play out most often during dating coaching. On the one hand, the people in my clients' lives are very, very opinionated about dating and relationships. On the other hand, we have a 50% divorce rate in the United States. I coach my clients to stick with professional, research-backed advice as opposed to heeding the anecdotal advice of girlfriends or bowling buddies.

Here are some things to consider about the effect of your social environment on your long-term change project:

- As human beings, we all need *validation*, which is just a fancy way of saying we need feedback from others indicating that we're on track, not too terribly weird, and not certifiably crazy.

- In any group of people, there will be pressure to conform for various reasons, the top two being that your change requires some uncomfortable effort from others, or that your change results in them questioning their own decisions, actions, and beliefs. So if your change effort feels hard because of the grief you're getting from those around you, that's a normal, highly likely byproduct of change.

- In my Life & Career Coaching practice, I've noticed that people can feel very intense abandonment anxiety whenever they sense possible rejection from a cherished group—I call this the *being kicked out of my tribe* phenomenon. My theory is that this is an evolutionary, hardwired reaction left over from tribal times, when being forced to go it alone in the wilderness often meant death. If you encounter this unique type of dread, use Self Talk to discuss how the feeling of threat doesn't match the actual level of danger in today's world, and how you now have the ability to "find your own tribe" within our much larger society.

- You can use group pressure to your advantage. Participation in a *support group* can give you feedback and encouragement from people who share your goals. That's why 12-step and weight-loss programs often stress the importance of group meetings. If there isn't a structured group to join, find a buddy or three who want to make the same change you do, meet regularly, and support each other.

- If you anticipate that significant people in your life will react negatively to your change, you may want to plan for that during the TTM Preparation stage. In particular, you may want to make some *contingency plans*. A contingency plan means that you prepare alternate courses of action. For example, you can plan to enroll a few trusted friends to support you before telling potentially non-supportive family and friends.

- Once your loved ones and friends see that the change is working well for you and that you're happy, the social pressure usually decreases and often stops. *Give it time.*

As you can tell from several of the stories presented in the book so far, change doesn't always go quickly or follow a straight line. The next section discusses a way to set your expectations so that the change process doesn't disappoint you or lower your motivation to stay with the program.

THE ROLE OF TRIAL AND ERROR

When it comes to important projects, we humans like to feel reassured by a good plan before we take a single step into action. Now on the one hand, I find that plans are very helpful. They set a direction, structure some activity, provide a bit of initial motivation, and get us off the couch and moving. On the other hand, it's hard to formulate a really good strategy without jumping in and getting some initial experience to inform that plan.

Consider this:

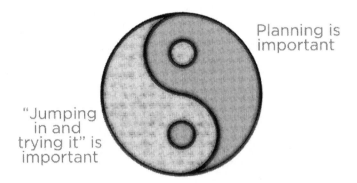

Planning is important

"Jumping in and trying it" is important

Let me share a story about the tension between planning and doing.

For more than 20 years, I was a software technical writer, designing and writing information to assist use of computer programs.

I remember that, back in the 1980s, it took software engineers a year or two to plan, code, test, and ship computer software. That process worked well enough at the time, but despite long and intense planning, there were often problems. For example, by the time we shipped the finished product, the market had changed, our competitors had evolved, and our product was no longer up to date. Also, sometimes it was only after we'd shipped the product that we'd get great suggestions from customers; obviously, it would've been helpful to have known these preferences much earlier in the design process.

So in the 1990s, software engineering changed. We began using an expedited process called *rapid prototyping*, which is just a fancy term for cycling through planning-and-doing very quickly (a precursor to the Agile movement and Scrum). We'd create a little bit, show what we had to customers, and then factor in their feedback before creating a little bit more. Repeat until the product is finished and the customers are happy. You can think of this process as giving the customers a chance to design and build the product along with the engineers.

As a result of this change, software products made it to market much faster—as fast as 6 months sometimes—and customer satisfaction went way up.

The business concept of *the pivot* is similar in the way it uses the synergy between planning and action. Eric Ries, the creator of the Lean Startup methodology, and other business analysts have noticed that the most successful start-up companies don't develop in a straight line from inspiration to business plan to success. Instead, the leaders of these businesses use what they've learned in the first few years to make a significant change to the company's strategic direction, one more likely to reap greater success.

A *pivot* is a significant change in strategic direction, metaphorically keeping one foot firmly planted while swinging the other foot to alter the course of the business.[40] The basic idea is that business success does not depend on sticking to the original plan as much as it requires making an informed, timely, major shift exactly when it's needed.

A great example of a business pivot is Groupon, which is a web-based marketing service that allows companies to offer email coupons for discounted products and services.

Originally, Groupon was an organization called The Point, which was a web-based service allowing activists to schedule and draw people to events; this original plan was not hugely successful. Almost on a whim, The Point offered a coupon for a pizzeria located in their office building, and they noticed that a significant percentage of their website viewers actually used it. They then pivoted the company toward online coupons, and the rest is history.[41]

So, hopefully I've convinced you that trial and error are an important part of any successful change process, and that's as true for individuals as it is for the largest and most successful businesses. *Chapter 5: Let's look at Pivot Points* in Part II explains in more detail how to use pivoting to further your change projects. Here are some things to consider about how trial-and-error activities can help your efforts:

- To be creative, it's helpful to *relax and be playful*, and "working to plan" usually crushes this spirit. When you're in a playful, creative state, your mind makes connections rapidly, moves toward pleasure, and produces entertaining results. If you can please yourself in this playful state, it's highly likely that your work will please others.

- Instead of experiencing *analysis paralysis*—being so overwhelmed by planning that you never take action—it's better to do something and learn from what happens.

- A trial-and-error approach can help you discover *what you don't want*, which can be a very helpful part of the process. Thomas Edison once said about initial attempts to invent the light bulb, *I have not failed. I've just found 10,000 ways that won't work.*[42]

- It can take a lot of practice to develop a skill, and it can take a lot of skill to create *something great*. Apply trial and error during your practice sessions, and then take what you've learned into the game, contest, or final presentation.

Many of the actions we take are habitual, and these habits may be serving needs other than advancing your change efforts. The next section reminds us of challenging habits and how we might manage them.

THE ROLE OF HABITS

Chapter 2: Let's look at habits explains the power of habits. This section summarizes the interplay between habits, the TTM change process, and managing your environment.

To start, let's acknowledge again that habits drive much of our behavior, with some studies suggesting that they drive up to 40% of our daily actions.[43]

Regarding the overall change process and its environment, we may face challenging habits of our own such as these:

- Having trouble saying no

- Submitting too quickly to authority

- Resisting authority

- Being a people pleaser

- Disliking groups

- Avoiding potential rejection

- Avoiding conflict

- Personalizing too much

- Blaming others

- Monopolizing the spotlight

- Failing to give others credit

- Not admitting you made a mistake

- Losing your temper

When something cues a habit (for example, a parent asks you to do something), you automatically launch into your routine (you say yes), and you get your reward (smooth relationships, avoidance of conflict). Saying no in this one particular instance might have been the best strategy for your change project, but the more advanced, thinking parts of your brain were shut off, and choice was unavailable to you; habits put you on automatic pilot.

So, it's challenging to avoid unhelpful habits that pull you off course, and it's also a challenge to take effective action consistently enough until it becomes your new, stronger habit. As you make your way through the TTM stages of change and as you interact with your environment, you're probably going to be bumping up against unhelpful habits with regularity.

While surfing the Internet recently, I encountered an unattributed quote that speaks to this challenge:

Live less out of habit and more out of intent

In my opinion, this quote almost gets it right. It's not that we need to live less out of habit, because habits are vitally important and necessary. More to the point is that we should not live out of habit when it's undermining our success. The issue is not amount, but timing.

The ticket out of Unhelpful Habit Land is to slow yourself, quiet down, and reconnect with your intentions. This process pulls you out of an automatic habit and re-engages the more advanced parts of your brain. At this point, you have access to choice again.

The ticket into *Helpful* Habit Land is to use a combination of structure, motivation, commitment, and tuning into intentions as a way to get you to do something consistently enough until it can become a new habit.

If you're thinking *Easier said than done!*, then fear not. First, it's not easy, but it's very, very do-able. Second, *Daily Pivots* provides you with some tools to help you access choice.

The next section reviews topics discussed in this chapter and gives you some food-for-thought before moving on to the next chapter.

LET'S SUM IT UP

Many of our change efforts—losing weight, exercising, transitioning a career, finding a compatible partner, saving money to buy a house—are *long-term projects*. Habit changes also require focused, organized, and sustained effort *over time*.

For an ongoing project, it's helpful to have a plan with a clear sense of priorities: for example, which goals need to be completed in the short term and which ones can be saved for later? Also, you're probably conducting your change effort among family members, coworkers, friends, neighbors, and members of society at large, all of whom will have opinions—sometimes *rather strong opinions*—about what you should be doing. Your ability to manage people and your emotional reactions will be important to the success of your project.

Also, as they say, life is what happens to you while you're busy making other plans.[44] So, it's helpful to accommodate some trial and error, and to be easy going about turning "mistakes" into successful plans for the future. There's much to be learned from a misstep or a relapse. Groupon never would've happened if the company gave up after The Point.

When managing your change project, you're faced with a choice that's similar to the one encountered when managing motivation. With motivation, you can either put large amounts of effort into creating a structure and a set of habits that support positive feelings about your project, or you can learn to refocus on *your intention* and slip back into its groove. Similarly, you can either create and adhere to a very large, structured, and detailed project plan for your change, or you can learn to relax and focus in a way that leaves you open to making good choices on the fly, moment to moment.

To avoid the pull of an unhelpful habit, you need awareness, good decision making, and a willingness to pivot into an action that supports your change effort. *PART II, JUST GET TO THE POINT ALREADY!*, provides you with great tools that you can use to pivot often and well.

◆ ◆ ◆

PART II: JUST GET TO THE POINT ALREADY!

To break free from an unhelpful habit that's got you in its grips, you need to recognize that you're slipping into the habit in a given moment, engage in some helpful Self Talk, and convince yourself to take more constructive action right then and there.

This part of the book describes the *Daily Pivots* method and provides stories designed to inspire you to do right by yourself and the goals you set. Pivot Inspiration stories are organized by the challenge or concern you're currently facing.

Here are the chapters in Part II:

- *Chapter 5: Let's look at Pivot Points*— Helps you understand the use of Pivot Inspirations to avoid unhelpful habits and to swing instead toward the change you want.

  The remaining chapters are organized by the unhelpful habit you want to overcome.

- *Being patient*

- *Boosting confidence*

- *Calming anxiety and fear*

- *Changing unhelpful beliefs*

- *Competing*

- *Enjoying the journey of life*

- *Focusing*

- *Letting go of control*

- *Making decisions*

- *Managing anger*

- *Reducing jealousy*

- *Relaxing about mistakes*

- *Taking better care of yourself*

- *Trying something different*

Each Pivot Inspiration story includes a link back to its category (for example, *Go back to Taking better care of yourself*).

Chapter 5: Let's look at Pivot Points

OK, you're motivated to make your big change—for example, finding that compatible spouse, improving your grades, starting a new business, or losing weight—and you've decided to make it *an important personal project.*

On some days and especially at first, it'll be easy to remember what to do, and you'll even feel like doing it! Once in a while, you may need a memory jog or a motivational boost—post-it notes on the refrigerator, attendance at a support group, calendar reminders—but generally you're on board...*you've gotten with the program.*

In cases like this, it's as if you're on a smooth journey in your car, moving easily from highway to highway, gliding along toward your destination. You're exactly where you should be, doing precisely what you need to do. There's no need to alter the course. Just...*carry on!*

Then there are *the other days,* times when *it's hard* to do the right thing. Maybe you're rushing, worrying, feeling stressed, or suffering from a cold or lack of sleep. Perhaps you're feeling the strong urge to nap or play video games instead of studying for your test or completing your resume. Or maybe you're *really hungry* and the fast-food drive-through window calls your name *like a siren song.*

At moments like these, it's as if you've gotten momentarily distracted from your journey, and *you're just about to miss the exit you need.* If you don't adjust in time, you'll speed right past it. At times like this, you need to refocus, hustle a little bit to position yourself, and pivot off the unhelpful path, back onto the one leading toward success.

This chapter is designed to provide you with practical tools for resisting wrong and doing right. Its sections include:

- *Defining pivot terms*—Learn the meaning of pivot, Pivot Points, Pivot Stories, and Pivot Inspirations.

- *"Has the jury reached a verdict?"*—Learn the primary Pivot Story used to activate all of the others.

- *Using the Courtroom Drama Pivot Story*—Read an example of using a Pivot Inspiration that convinces your jury to decide in favor of change instead of the unhelpful habit.

- *Let's sum it up*—Let's review before you move on to using Pivot Inspirations.

Defining Pivot Terms

The previous section described being dragged too far down the highway, putting you at risk for missing the exit you need to stay on track with your change project. To succeed, you need to pivot off onto that exit.

A *pivot* is a change in direction, and this book uses pivoting as a metaphor for course correction. To pivot, at some point while walking in a straight line, you plant one foot, swing your other foot out and around, and set off again at a different angle, like this:

I'm recommending a *personal pivot*, one in which you stop moving in the direction of an unhelpful habit and pivot instead in the direction of the change you want. When you adjust like this often enough, you successfully reach your goals, and adjusting in that new direction eventually becomes more habitual—easier and more automatic.

Originally, a pivot described a physical motion; I'm most familiar with it from playing the center position on my high school basketball team. Basketball players use an abrupt change in direction and a swing of the leg to avoid a defender, giving themselves more space to score.

Daily Pivots are more verbal and emotional; instead of swinging your leg, you use Self Talk to swing your attention, your focus. You come at the situation mentally from a different angle in a way that relaxes you, and in a way that boosts both motivation and ability to perform well.

A *Pivot Story* is a Self-Talk conversation—a self-administered *pep talk*—that convinces you to avoid old behaviors and to pivot into change. I usually use the term *Pivot Inspiration* to describe these stories, because their main purpose is to inspire you to do the right thing in a given moment.

A *Pivot Point* is a moment when you're being pulled along by an old habit, yet there's still time to apply a Pivot Inspiration to alter your course. Previous chapters have described situations that can make it hard to detect Pivot Points— speedy thoughts and internal processing, doing too many things too quickly, responding to fear, surrendering to comfort, or feeling the emotional tug of an old habit. Dedicating yourself to slowing down and observing yourself will serve you will as you learn to pivot.

The next section describes a central Pivot Story, which provides the "jumping off point" for all the other Pivot Inspirations in the rest of this book.

"HAS THE JURY REACHED A VERDICT?"

As a Life & Career Coach, I often help struggling clients to analyze times when they've recently gotten off track. So, I've heard many detailed stories about how this feels for them.

Clients report that there's often an initial rationalization that they're about to get off track; for example, *I'll just check my email before I begin working. That won't take long, and I'll get right to it when I'm finished.* They also report that the unhelpful habit kicks into gear without much conscious thought. For example, checking email quickly shifts into visiting websites which segues smoothly into online shopping which devolves into video game playing. *Hours disappear!*

I'll often ask my clients if they were completely unaware of getting off track, as if the intended task completely slipped their minds. Almost all of them say no. They report a vague awareness of the undone task. Regardless, by that time, the unhelpful habit has built up such a strong momentum that it's hard to break free.

Finally, when I get my clients to provide the most honest description of their feelings when they are deep in the clutches of the unhelpful habit, they say that they *feel like* continuing the unhelpful behavior, and they *just don't feel like* taking the better course of action. *Period.*

It's as if a decision-making process has concluded. Yet, like an iceberg in ocean water, you're consciously aware of only a tiny portion of it above the surface, yet most of the decision-making process is taking place in deeply submerged, subconscious waters.

To get out of this trap, you need to find a way to raise this process completely into your conscious awareness so that you can alter the outcome. In these moments, applying some dry Self Talk or reciting a single, sugary affirmation won't get the job done. You need something stronger, more emotionally compelling, something more deeply convincing.

*   *   *

Let me introduce a very powerful Pivot Story you can use to  affect change. Let's call it the *Courtroom Drama Pivot Story.*

Immediately before you automatically launch into an unhelpful habit, it's as if a courtroom drama is happening just beneath your awareness. To get a sense of the scene, think of the second half of any episode of the TV show *Law & Order,* or you can think of your favorite legal movie. (*The truth? You can't* **handle** *the truth!*)

134

The key participants in this courtroom drama are very familiar: the Judge, the Jury, the Prosecuting Attorney, and the Defense Attorney. In real life, this subconscious trial of ours happens in a split second. However, I'm going to slow it all down so you can understand how it plays out just under the surface of your awareness. Also, remember that *you are all of the participants.* You're the Judge who makes sure that everyone plays by the rules, you're the Attorneys who make the arguments, and you're the Jury who renders the final decision.

As you'll recall from your favorite courtroom dramas, the opening and closing statements from the Attorneys are done with flair. They might raise their voices, use props, wax poetic, pace, point, and gesture passionately with their arms; it's not a dry speech with only logical facts. The Attorneys' job is to create *an emotional argument* that will touch the heart or hit the gut. They need to compel the Jury—*compel them*—to decide in their favor. It's dramatic, and it's intense.

So when you're launching into an unhelpful habit, it's as if your Prosecuting Attorney has just given a *great* speech to the Jury, and they're buying it. For example, if you're a procrastinator, then the Prosecuting Attorney just delivered an intensely emotional and effective argument for procrastinating. If you're a perfectionist, then she delivered a knockout argument for striving for perfection.

Remember that your Prosecuting Attorney is arguing for *your unhelpful habit.*

Now as you know, despite a great performance by the Prosecuting Attorney, the Defense Attorney gets a chance to deliver a rebuttal, a counter argument. It's at this point in the courtroom drama that things get interesting. You may think, *Wow that Prosecuting Attorney sure sounded convincing. I think she's guilty.* Then after the Defense Attorney gives an equally powerful opening statement, you might think, *Darn. Now I'm not so sure...both arguments sound pretty good.*

Remember that your Defense Attorney is arguing for *the change you want.*

In an average courtroom drama, we know who's guilty ahead of time, and we're just waiting to see if justice prevails. In a *great* courtroom drama, the case is complicated, and we're unsure about the outcome. Sometimes, the Defense Attorney must address, debate, and shoot down the Prosecuting Attorney's arguments. Sometimes, she must take a truth revealed by the Prosecuting Attorney and expand upon it, so the jury can understand *the whole truth.*

So, it's time in this courtroom drama for the Defense Attorney to knock down the argument for the unhelpful habit and to give a compelling reason for change. Now, imagine the camera panning across the courtroom, and we see the Defense Attorney....

...sound asleep at her table.

In this example, the Defense Attorney was completely absent, and failed to deliver any rebuttal or counter argument. The members of the Jury shake their heads in disbelief and have no choice but to decide for the prosecution: *let's procrastinate!* or *let's be a perfectionist!* In situations like this, your Judge should wake up your Defense Attorney, charge her with contempt, and boot her out of the courtroom. Your Judge needs to bring in a competent, ethical Defense Attorney.

It's also possible that the Defense Attorney is awake and doing her job, but she's delivering a weak argument. Let me give you a brief example. I was using this Courtroom Pivot Story during a meeting with a client who procrastinates, and I asked him to imagine a great, compelling argument that would convince his Jury to stop avoiding and get on with it. He gave this reply in a soft, meek voice: *Well...errr...umm...I guess...I guess I'd be better off if I just got it done.*

True, that. But will that argument convince a Jury? Most likely not.

Remember that his Prosecuting Attorney had just delivered a knockout, passionate speech. There was emotion, finger pointing, high energy, hand waving, and props...*if the glove does not fit, YOU MUST ACQUIT!!!* Next, imagine the mousy Defense Attorney shuffling up to the jury box and then responding with this: *well...errr...umm...I guess...I guess I'd be better off if I just got it done.*

Which argument do you think feels more intensely compelling to the Jury? No contest. His Jury will decide to keep procrastinating.

So, this is *your* personal courtroom drama that we're talking about. What are *you* going to do with it? How will you allow it to play out?

> *Using the Daily Pivot method, you'll be providing your Defense Attorney with a Pivot Inspiration, which will undercut the argument of the Prosecuting Attorney and will convince your Jury to work toward your desired change. This is structured Self Talk designed to get you to resist your old habit and act in a way that lines up with your intention to change.*

Keep experimenting with Defense-Attorney arguments until you're able to stop yourself from getting off track in the moment and are able to pivot into change. Do this often enough, and you've just formed a healthy, new habit.

At this point, some of you might be thinking *easier said than done.* Although you'd be right, here are some points to consider:

- It may not be easy, but it's easier than it seems at first glance.

- If easy approaches worked—such as dry, canned Self Talk or trite affirmations—I wouldn't have needed an *entire book* to get this information to you. I would have tossed it off in a blog post, like everyone else tries to do.

- It's easier than the consequences of remaining a slave to your unhelpful habits, moods, and comforts.

- If you practice and take it one day at a time, it'll get easier and easier. If you do it often enough for it to become an automatic habit, then *it gets **really** easy.*

Despite the fact that implementing *Daily Pivots* takes time, here's some heartening news. When you first start using *Daily Pivots*, you don't have to be awesomely convincing. All you need is to generate a *willingness to do the right thing* in that moment. Create one "small win" today and then again tomorrow, and stronger motivation eventually follows.

The next section provides an example of how to use Pivot Inspirations to convince your Jury to render a decision for change.

Using the Courtroom Drama Pivot Story

Being the sneaky author that I am, I've already given you some examples of using Pivot Inspirations. The first one is the story I told at the very beginning of the *Forward* that describes my Zen Driving project. That story is a more personalized version of the *No harm, no foul* Pivot Inspiration in the *Managing anger* chapter.

Here's how you can see an opportunity to pivot and take advantage of it:

1. Notice when you're feeling upset, feeling the urge to lapse into an unhelpful habit, or actually beginning to lapse.

   Mindfulness skills greatly improve your ability to do this (see *Appendix A: Let's look at mindfulness*)

2. Take a deep breath, exhale, and slow your thinking and actions.

   If you're able, get up, take a walk, get away from the computer screen, look out the window, and take a two-minute break; just breathe and be in your body. It's at this point that you've interrupted that rapid slide into your old habit. (For information about taking mini-breaks like these, see the *How to "slip into a groove" without motivation* section in *Chapter 3: Let's look at Motivation.*)

3. Remember the Courtroom Drama Pivot Story.

   No need to go over it in detail, just recall it briefly. Remind yourself that your Prosecuting Attorney just had his turn, which resulted in the urge to lapse into the old habit. It's now your Defense Attorney's turn, and he needs to make the most of it.

   At this point, I like to say in my own use of Self Talk, *OK, it's time for us to have a little chat.*

4. Tell your Jury a story selected from the Pivot Inspirations presented in this part of the book.

Select a Self-Talk story based on the challenge that you're facing. If your old habit is tugging you toward panic because you're facing a tough decision, then you can try one of the Pivot Inspirations in the *Making decisions* chapter. If competition is unnerving you at the moment, then you can try telling yourself a story from the *Competing* chapter.

You can tell the story any way you want. You can read it verbatim from this book. You can tell part of it or all of it. You can change it, adding examples from your life. Finally, you can sum it up using a simple phrase such as *no harm, no foul*. You can think through as little or as much as it takes until you decide to abandon the old habit and pivot into change.

Remember that it's not **the story's** *responsibility to convince you to resist your old habit and to change; it's* **the story teller's** *responsibility.* It's **your** responsibility.

So, experiment and practice; develop your story telling skills until you're able to motivate your audience (you). Become your own best storyteller.

5. Ask yourself, *What's my intention?*
    Remind yourself of what you hope to gain from your change project. Ask yourself what kind of man or

woman do you want to be after all is said and done? How do you want to be about this?

6. Choose change instead of the old habit, clear your mind, and then relax and concentrate as you put your decision into action. You don't have to be wildly motivated; you just need to be **willing** to get back on track and to do the right thing.

For example, if you avoided procrastination and got busy with the task you were avoiding, give that task your entire attention and energy. Focus on it, and really get into it. Almost every time, your emotions will fall into place and support what you've decided to do. Motivation frequently **follows** a little bit of action.

Let's look at a few examples of how I might pivot from getting angry in traffic into feeling peaceful, patient, compassionate, and willing to cooperate with other drivers. For each of these examples, assume that I used my mindfulness skills to notice I was about to lose my temper in traffic, I was able to take a deep breath and exhale, I react well to humor, and I remembered being positively motivated (see the *How does motivation work?* section in *Chapter 3: Let's talk about motivation* for more information).

For Self Talk, this is what my Defense Attorney could say to my Jury:

> *OK, Gerry. You know the drill, sir. I know you want to get angry at these drivers and try to get them to move along faster and drive better just*

*by sheer force of your will. You think the traffic should cater to you? I wish! "I'M KING OF THE WORLD," or at least I SHOULD be. Anyhow...there's no law that says that I have to get there any quicker than it's going to take. I can't force everyone to drive the way I WANT them to drive. What I CAN do it go with the flow here. I know how to avoid the crazies by staying in the middle lane. I know what it's like to back off a wavering driver in the lane next to me, giving him plenty of space to cut across a few lanes and dart off the exit. I know how great it can feel to put my peace of mind at the top of my priority list, focusing on music from the radio, feeling my butt in the seat and my grip on the wheel, noticing the sky and clouds, checking out the cars and trees and houses as I pass on by. **I'll get there when I get there.** As long as I go with the flow and do what I've learned to give others space, then...hey...there's no harm being done here. I can groove with this. Relax and focus and enjoy the ride. I'll get there when I get there. **No harm, no foul**, right?*

Good...good! [pause] *OK, sir. What is your intention moving forward? What kind of man do you want to be right here and now? How do you want to be about this? What do you have to do so that you're proud of yourself when you've completed this drive? Your choice, my man.*

Perhaps a shorter version might work on another day:

143

Go with the flow. Just like on the basketball court. Drive to the hoop. I got fouled, but who cares? Call the foul, slow the game down, piss everyone off...no way! That's no fun. Just roll with it. If it doesn't stop you from making the basket, then let it go. **Let it go!** *Play on. Enjoy the game. My car's fine. I'm fine. Life's fine. No harm, no foul...***No harm, no foul!**

So, how do I want to be about this?

On another given day, this might work:

Hey. **No harm, no foul.** *mmm-hmm!*

Different problems will require different Self-Talk conversations; some are longer, some are shorter, some are funnier, and some are firmer in tone. Convincing your Jury to  relax instead of getting angry might require a certain kind of talk. Convincing the jury to stop procrastinating and to get on with a task may require a conversation with a different emphasis or tone.

This is a *respectful conversation* that you're having with yourself over time. The trial might be a quick one, or it might be one of those federal cases that play out over many months. Don't let one bad day of Self Talk discourage you. Play the long game, and keep the conversation going. Eventually, you'll convince your Jury, because the pull toward being your best self is stronger than everything else, as long as you stay focused over time.

Keep experimenting with Self Talk that gets you back on track quickly. Work with a coach, therapist, support group, or friends who understand pivoting and who can give you helpful feedback for your Defense Attorney. Practice Defense-Attorney arguments and pay attention to ones that work, for you and for other people.

Once you find conversations that work, use them often. As you get better and better at talking yourself back on track, you'll get closer and closer to a new, automatic habit. It's only a matter of time before you're doing it without much conscious thought and you're staying on track.

The next section reviews topics discussed in this chapter and gives you some food-for-thought before moving on to the Pivot Inspirations contained in the rest of this book.

LET'S SUM IT UP

 Children love stories. When I think about this, my mind immediately goes to the classics my parents read to me at bedtime. Yet, there were other wonderful times and places for storytelling, perhaps curled up on the couch with an aunt or uncle, or an older brother or sister. Maybe you heard stories

in the car during a family trip or sitting on a blanket while picnicking. Stories may have been read from a book, told in song, seen on a video, presented in a game, or sprung from the minds of the storyteller himself.

The combination of your youthful imagination and the comforting presence of a loved one *created magic*. It was a way to explore the world—or distant worlds—from the safe embrace of your family, your home, your bed. It was a way to try something wildly new while being physically rooted in the familiar. It was a way of testing and trying new things in your mind before having to take any action or face risk. It was a way for you to imagine being a brave hero while being comforted by the *real* hero in your life, *the storyteller*.

The potent mix of imagination, comfort, safety, learning, and belief in the story lingers for years, even decades. When Hollywood released an imaginative live-  action version of the children's story *Where the Wild Things Are*, adults like me were thrilled all over again. In addition to fond memories from childhood, its lessons resonated with my adult self as well.

Indeed, storytelling isn't just for kids. We adults turn to TV, blogs and vlogs, plays, video games, poems, songs, and film. Themes from these stories can become very personal lessons that we carry individually, or they can become part of our cultural fabric. As one minor example, after the movie *Jerry*

Maguire became popular a few decades ago, the phrase "you complete me" became a familiar part of our lives. Nearly twenty years later, hearing that phrase often evokes strong emotions that amuse, move, and sometimes guide us.

Stories can *inspire us* like no other form of communication. They have that ability to touch our hearts, challenge our minds, focus us, and motivate us to act. They can touch all parts of our humanity simultaneously, and they remind us of who we used to be, who we are, and who we hope to become. When we take action from that place, we are very, *very* powerful beings.

*   *   *

Now is the time for you to become your own best storyteller, *your own hero.* When you detect yourself sliding off track, failing to honor the goals you set for yourself, it's up to *you* to swoop in and save the day.

Convince yourself to stay the course, to continue along the path of building your happiest, most successful life. Your desire to act will come from a well-told story that makes sense, *moves you,* inspires deep belief, and compels you to do what *you need to do* in that moment.

Give that Pivot Story to your Defense Attorney, and watch her knock the socks off your Jury. Practice often, see her skill increase, and *watch* as you become ***your own best self.***

Being patient

Pivot away from impatience and into patience.

Pivot Inspirations:

- *Getting in the house* (page 150)

- *It's like a jigsaw puzzle* (page 154)

- *Making your way through a maze* (page 156)

- *Therapy for an atrophied limb* (page 158)

- *Untying a horribly knotted shoelace* (page 160)

- *You start in little league, not in the majors* (page 163)

Getting in the house

Defense Attorney's story for your Jury...

Sometimes we feel as if we're on the outside of something looking in; we want to be included, to have a sense that *we've arrived* and can relax. That inside destination could be career advancement, getting married, building a larger circle of friends, or some other important   personal goal.

At times like this, it can sometimes feel as if you've made a reasonable attempt to get into a house, and, after failing a few times, you want to walk back to the street and give up.

For example, knocking on the front and back doors are as far as most of us would think of going. It's our hope that its occupants will answer our call and let us in. If that doesn't happen, then the door remains locked, we're left on the outside, and we feel frustrated, at a loss. Many of us would give up at this point, and for good reason given common courtesy and legalities.

However, let's assume it's *urgent* that we get into that house, that one way or another, we *HAVE* to make that happen. I know that what I'm proposing is exaggerated and extreme, but I promise that it'll make sense to you by the time the story ends. Hang in there with me....

So, as mentioned, our first attempts at the front and back doors failed. Nonetheless, one way or the other, we're going to get in there. It's time to get outside our comfort zone and try something different.

For example, we can try the windows. A sibling of mine who will remain nameless spent a good portion of her teenage years forgetting her house keys and climbing through the unlocked windows of our house. It's not particularly polite, and, if you don't live there, it's illegal. Yet, under certain circumstances, it can work. To quote a former colleague's email signature, *Perfect is the enemy of done*[45].

Let's keep getting creative, because maybe all the windows are locked. Let's not get too ahead of ourselves and think in terms of busting down the door or breaking windows. Those options are open to us later, but let's take a look at a few other ways we could gain entrance.

If the house has a cellar or garage, we may be able to get into the house through a door there. In days of old, climbing down the chimney like Santa Clause might have been an option. Maybe we tried only the windows on the ground floor, and using a ladder to enter the windows on the upper floors is a possibility.

If you're more conservative, maybe you'll wait for the owners to get home before asking for entrance. Or maybe you can make friends with the owners over time and eventually receive an invitation.

If you're more radical, have huge disposable income, or have no fear of jail, we could break in. In an extreme case, we can take a backhoe to the side of the house and get in that way, disregarding the massive damage we're doing to the poor house. Too bad! Remember, we're going to get in there one way or another.

On the one hand, given the degree of difficulty, it would be very reasonable to decide to give up on getting into the house. On the other hand, *let's not pretend that it's impossible.* If you want it badly enough, and if you can accept consequences for certain actions, there's *ALWAYS* a way into the house. Where there's a will, there's a way.

*   *   *

The next time you become impatient and negative after a few initial failed attempts, relax and remind yourself of this story about different ways to get into a house. Find a way to approach the situation that matches your values and whose consequences you can accept, and give it some creativity and effort over time.

Don't let pride stand in your way of something that you feel must get done. If busting a window only to have to pay for its repair later is the only way in, then accept that consequence and pay the price. If getting dirty while sliding down the chimney is the only way in, then wreck your clothes and get it done.

Finally, don't forget that you don't have to go it alone; your best option may be to enlist some help and support from others. It's a lot easier to gain entrance with the assistance of the occupants than it is to go it alone.

Now, make that final plea to your Jury...

Feel this story's truth. Clear your mind, and breathe deeply. Now ask yourself: *What kind of person do I intend to be right now? What do I need to do to feel proud of myself when I'm done?*

Continue breathing deeply — Make a decision — Act!

*Back to **Being patient** (page 149)*

It's like a jigsaw puzzle

Defense Attorney's story for your Jury...

When first beginning to work on a change project, it's common for my clients to feel frustrated—sometimes *panicky*—when an initial attempt doesn't work.

When this happens, I say they should approach their project as if putting together a jigsaw puzzle.

All the pieces are in the box, so you know ahead of time that success is inevitable; with enough time, effort, and patience, it will all come together. So...you might as well *relax and have fun.*

If you pick up any two jigsaw puzzle pieces, it's highly unlikely that they'll fit. Think of how bizarre it would be for someone to attempt to put two random puzzle pieces together, fail, and then freak out about it: *I failed! There's no way this puzzle will ever come together!!!* Panicking creates chaos and wastes time.

Now on the one hand, you could hold one puzzle piece in your hand and attempt to fit it into every other piece of the puzzle. That strategy would work *eventually*, but it would be *boring*.

Instead, if you relax, engage your curiosity and imagination, and take a more *playful approach* to the activity, maybe you can find additional clever, interesting, and fun ways to put the puzzle together. For example, maybe you can start by placing all of the pieces together that have a smooth edge and using them to construct the border. Or maybe you can group pieces together that have a similar color, and then use the picture on the box to guide your efforts.

But it's all good. Just notice the irony that patiently relaxing and having fun usually leads to completing a task faster. *Funny*, that!

Now, make that final plea to your Jury...

Feel this story's truth. Clear your mind, and breathe deeply. Now ask yourself: *What kind of person do I intend to be right now? What do I need to do to feel proud of myself when I'm done?*

Continue breathing deeply — Make a decision — Act!

*Back to **Being patient** (page 149)*

Making your way through a maze

One of the most challenging things you can do is attempt to navigate a very complex maze. Given that, I heard an intriguing fact recently. Someone said that, if you place your  hand on either the right or left wall in a maze and never lift it as you travel the corridors, you'll eventually find your way out of the maze. When I imagined doing that, it made sense why this is a sure-fire way to go.

Of course if you use this method, you'll be traveling down many dead-end pathways. This technique is also highly likely to take you along one of the longest routes to the exit. Despite the negatives, if you use this strategy, you *will* find your way out of the maze. *It's just a matter of time.*

Now when I work with my Life & Career Coaching clients, I emphasize having fun, and I'm aware that many people would find such a mechanical solution to be mind-numbingly dull. So if entertaining yourself is a higher priority than taking the surest route, then go have fun, experiment, use other methods, and find a more interesting way to make your way through the corridors. Otherwise, you can always fall back on what's *guaranteed* to work.

*   *   *

What I like best about this example is that it just goes to show you that, if you're patient enough and have the right strategy, *success is guaranteed.* Just relax and give your plan time to play itself out.

Now, make that final plea to your Jury...

Feel this story's truth. Clear your mind, and breathe deeply. Now ask yourself: *What kind of person do I intend to be right now? What do I need to do to feel proud of myself when I'm done?*

Continue breathing deeply — Make a decision — Act!

Back to ***Being patient*** *(page 149)*

Therapy for an atrophied limb

Defense Attorney's story for your Jury...
Years ago, I watched a quirky fantasy movie called *The Lady in the Water*. Much of the action took place near a pool in an apartment complex and included an assortment of *very odd* characters.

One person was a muscle builder who insisted on using only one of his arms to lift weights, leading to a very extreme appearance. One arm was enormous and bulging with muscle, as you would expect to see on any professional body builder. The other arm was average sized, as you would expect on a man who never lifted weights.

If you assessed the normal sized arm alone in terms of its look and how it functioned, you'd definitely conclude that it was a normal, healthy arm. Though, if you compared the average arm to the enormously-built arm, you'd probably find it lacking and inferior.

It's not that there's anything *wrong* with the smaller arm. What's wrong is the imbalance. Lift enough weight with the *smaller arm*, and in time, it will be able to do everything the gigantic arm can do today.

*   *   *

When my Life & Career Coaching clients struggle because of a lack of skill, they often conclude that there's something wrong with them, and this self-criticism erodes confidence, feels painful, and leads to avoidance. This reaction makes the situation worse, because avoidance guarantees that skill will remain low.

Instead, I encourage my clients to view the lack of skill in the same way that they might look at an atrophied, under-developed limb. Don't avoid using the limb out of fear. Instead, put the limb through physical therapy, and build up the degree of difficulty slowly. In due time, the atrophied limb will respond to the therapy, get stronger, and perform the way you want.

Approach any skill deficit in the same way. Work it out and build it up until it gives you the results you want.

Now, make that final plea to your Jury...
Feel this story's truth. Clear your mind, and breathe deeply. Now ask yourself: *What kind of person do I intend to be right now? What do I need to do to feel proud of myself when I'm done?*

Continue breathing deeply — Make a decision — Act!

*Back to **Being patient** (page 149)*

Untying a horribly knotted shoelace

Life is complicated, right? Sometimes you're not facing just one straightforward problem. Sometimes it's a few difficulties all conspiring together. There are other times when you know

 how to solve a problem, but there are several obstacles standing in your way, blocking your progress. When this happens, it's almost as if you're facing a horribly knotted shoelace.

We've all experienced those nasty knots. You're so used to giving a tug and having it all untie in one smooth, graceful motion. *But not this time.* You give a tug on the lace, it begins to untie as it usually does, and then...***STOP.***

Now if you're like me, you aren't being mindful right in that moment, so you do the worst possible thing: *you yank harder.* It doesn't work, of course. Yet you do it *again*, because you *think* it should work. As a result, you're faced with a knotted jumble, made tighter and all the more difficult to untie due to your hard, frustrated tugging and pulling.

At this point, you might sigh, swear, and end up pulling off your shoe to get a closer look at the mess you just made. The secret to dealing with this situation is to switch gears from rushing, yanking, getting angry, and being stubborn, to shifting into a sense of acceptance: accepting that this is going to take longer than you had originally planned, and that it's not going to be so easy this time. This isn't what you had in mind, but you can deal *just fine*.

Once you calm yourself and slow down, you begin work on the knot. You'll visually scan it, trying to find a loose bit of lace. Once you find that, you'll gently tug on it a few times to see if you can create some grip space, or you might move the lace side-to-side as a way to loosen it. More often than not, the first few times you try this will fail; the bit of shoe lace remains snug against the knot.

You make your way around the entire knot, tugging gently on various bits of lace. The second time around, bits of lace are slightly looser. *Progress!* Next, you'll notice that you occasionally find a bit of shoe lace that slides out into a sizable loop. **Major** *progress!*

When you've got some of the shoelace pulled out into loops, you then know you're very close. It's just a matter of finding out why one of these large loops won't pull all the way out, and you focus on untangling that one loop...and then another...and *another*.

Loop after loop, the knot unravels, and your shoe is finally untied. I've never actually timed it, but I would imagine that the whole horrible-knot-untying process takes a few minutes, tops. All in all, not bad!

*   *   *

The next time you get tangled up in a challenging, complex situation, and you feel the irritation, fear, and impatience building, think about what it takes to untie a bad shoelace knot. Get in touch with that feeling you get when finally accepting the problem instead of struggling impotently against it.

Slow down, and stop trying to force things. Try a few approaches. Be a good sport when your initial attempts don't yield immediate results, because it takes some gentle tugging and jiggling to get some grip space and some loosening. In time, you'll create one loose loop, and then it's only a matter of time before you completely untangle the situation.

Now, make that final plea to your Jury...
Feel this story's truth. Clear your mind, and breathe deeply. Now ask yourself: *What kind of person do I intend to be right now? What do I need to do to feel proud of myself when I'm done?*

Continue breathing deeply — Make a decision — Act!

Back to *Being patient* (page 149)

You start in little league, not in the majors

Defense Attorney's story for your Jury...

Let's imagine that a very little boy and his father are playing Wiffle Ball in the backyard. The boy shows a tremendous amount of interest and some natural aptitude for hitting and catching the ball. After they finish playing, the father runs the idea past his son about joining a baseball team, and the son is excited to give it a try.

Now, here's where the story gets ridiculously exaggerated to make a point. Stay with me, OK?

So instead of a Tee-ball league, the father takes his five-year-old son to a major league baseball team. You know, like the Baltimore Orioles, the Los Angeles Dodgers, or the Minnesota Twins. Miraculously, the manager decides to allow the boy onto the field to practice with the professionals.

Clearly, this story is absurd. A young child doesn't yet have the skill or maturity to play with professional adult baseball players. Not only would the child be unable to perform, but he might get seriously hurt or killed in the process.

This is not a statement about the boy's skill level; he may indeed be future big-league material. Still, he'll have to work his way up through the system: Tee-ball, Little League, high school and perhaps college ball, the minor leagues, and then the major leagues. If the boy is gifted enough to skip a level here or there, the coaches will make that judgment call.

*　　*　　*

I make a point to my Life & Career Coaching clients that two ways we make ourselves miserable is through *comparisons* and *expectations*. In many areas of life—career advancement, entrepreneurship, dating, exercising—people sometimes jump quickly into a too-complex project with very lofty expectations. When the early results don't come close to matching those expectations, my clients sometimes resort to blaming others, criticizing themselves harshly, or giving up.

Sometimes in life, we jump into a situation a little bit ahead of our skill level. Sometimes you have to go back down so that you can rise again later. Sometimes you have to take a few steps backward before you can move forward again. Lower the degree of difficulty, go research and practice and build your skill, and then return to the higher level when your ability is a match for the challenge.

Don't impatiently jump right into the major leagues. Be willing to start off in Little League, and work your way up.

Now, make that final plea to your Jury...
Feel this story's truth. Clear your mind, and breathe deeply. Now ask yourself: *What kind of person do I intend to be right now? What do I need to do to feel proud of myself when I'm done?*

Continue breathing deeply — Make a decision — Act!

Back to **Being patient** (page 149)

Boosting confidence

Pivot away from low self-esteem and doubt, and into confidence.

Pivot Inspirations:

- *Afraid of a weakness? Own and then transcend it!* (page 166)

- *Flip the switch* (page 169)

- *If others can do it, you can* (page 171)

- *Let the dog run, or make it heel* (page 174)

- *Practices should be harder than the games* (page 177)

- *Time travel conversation about driving* (page 180)

Afraid of a weakness? Own and then transcend it!

Spoiler alert: I reveal plot details from the movie *Fried Green Tomatoes.*

Early in the story, we witness the tragic death of the handsome, young Buddy Threadgoode. While attempting to retrieve Ruth Jamison's hat along the railroad tracks, his foot becomes stuck between two rails, and he's killed by an oncoming train. A good portion of the movie involves Ruth's struggle to recover from this trauma and return to enjoying life again.

Later, Ruth's son, Buddy Threadgoode Jr., is playing with his friends along the very same railroad tracks. We hear the screech of a train and people yelling. Of course, we fear that the son befell the same fate as his namesake.

Yet as the movie so often does, it lightens tragedy with comedy. The scene cuts to a funeral, but it's Buddy Jr's *arm* that's being buried, not the boy.

Consider this exchange:[46]

> **Ruth:** *I can understand having a funeral for an arm, I just don't know WHY she insists on calling him Stump.*
>
> **Sipsey:** *Miss Idgie says everyone else will be calling him that, we might as well be the first.*

The scene cuts to a brightly smiling, confident, one-armed boy running along the road with his buddies.

*   *   *

Sometimes, people experience a dip in confidence when their focus drifts *away* from what they can accomplish and *toward* some weakness or vulnerability. This distraction can become even more intense when someone fears public bullying, shaming, rejection, or humiliation.

As a shortcut around this difficult situation, acknowledge the weakness and own it in a matter-of-fact way. Grab the topic before one of your enemies can, speak of it with a *So what?* tone of voice, remove any emotional charge so it's no longer a shameful secret, and then move your focus to what you *can* do. In that last scene, Buddy Jr. was focusing on all the fun things a one-armed boy could do with his friends; the lack of an arm is beside the point.

Some social justice movements use this technique, and they call it *reclaiming the word.* So, a group will take a word formerly used to harass them, use it to refer to its own members, and change the meaning to something positive. The idea is to remove a painful verbal weapon from your bully's arsenal.

Not every application of this principle needs to be so personally heavy. For example, if a potential employer cites an employment gap or some other problematic part of your job history, own it briefly, point out any hidden benefit, and state briefly what you've learned from it and why you're still the best candidate for the position. Focus on what you *can* do, what you'll bring to the table.

If you are going to be hired into the position, the only winning strategy involves going down this path with a smile and confidence. "Not being afraid *to go there*" conveys confidence. Finally, if you don't feel particularly confident yet, then "fake it until you make it"; act confidently until you begin to *feel* confident later.

Now, make that final plea to your Jury...

Feel this story's truth. Clear your mind, and breathe deeply. Now ask yourself: *What kind of person do I intend to be right now? What do I need to do to feel proud of myself when I'm done?*

Continue breathing deeply — Make a decision — Act!

*Back to **Boosting confidence** (page 165)*

Flip the switch

Lack confidence? *That's OK.* There's something more important than confidence.

Really successful people don't often spend significant amounts of time gauging their confidence level or attempting to jack it up. They're too busy working.

You see, for successful people, there's a switch that gets flipped, and that switch is off (*I'm not going to do this*) or on (*I'm going to do this*).

It's not about *feeling*, it's about commitment. It's not about thinking into the future and predicting success; it's about fully engaging and performing *just today's tasks* successfully. (If things fail today, then it's about going back at it tomorrow and the next day until you succeed.) It's a commitment to do whatever it takes, *period*. Finally, it's about simultaneously being a good sport about *the possibility of failure* and choosing not to dwell on it until it happens.

Don't put the cart before the horse. Don't expect to feel confident before you begin working on your project. Flip on that switch, and decide to do it. Commit to the work, and confidence will come as you learn, develop, and make your way through your daily tasks.

Decide that, if others can do it, you can eventually learn how to do it as well. Decide that you'll figure it out over time and with effort. Decide to be patient and to recover from mistakes gracefully. Decide that you'll get help when needed. Decide to feed the desire and starve the fear. *Decide to **do it!***

If you want it, then flip that switch.

Now, make that final plea to your Jury...
Feel this story's truth. Clear your mind, and breathe deeply. Now ask yourself: *What kind of person do I intend to be right now? What do I need to do to feel proud of myself when I'm done?*

Continue breathing deeply — Make a decision — Act!

*Back to **Boosting confidence** (page 165)*

If others can do it, you can

Defense Attorney's story for your Jury...

In my Life & Career Coaching practice, clients share their hopes, dreams, and desires with me. When thinking about this, it's clear that their goals are most often common and attainable. Examples include wanting to graduate college, starting one's own business, reducing stress, finding a compatible partner, losing weight, getting a raise, owning a home, or maybe just taking a nice vacation.

I often coach my clients to network, to go have conversations with people who have already achieved these goals or who otherwise understand how it's done. Networking meetings provide great information and boost confidence. After all, if the person sitting across the table from you has done it, then you can probably do it, too.

For example, if you think that finding a compatible partner is beyond your reach, reflect on the people in your life who have partners. Are they filthy rich and gorgeous? Probably not. Stroll the mall and observe the couples. It's always remarkable to me the number of pairings you'd never anticipate based on looks alone. They look pretty much like you and me, right?

Are the people who own homes significantly smarter and more capable than you? Can you spot business owners who are reasonably successful yet who don't seem wildly more skilled or brighter than you? Do some research into how that person got the raise you wanted but didn't get. Are you capable of doing what she did to get the raise?

Remember, if other people of similar brain power and skill level can achieve these goals, then, clearly, *you can do it, too!*

*   *   *

Now, some of you might be wondering if it's possible to pick a goal that's out of reach given your natural ability. Yep, that can happen. For example, if I said it was my goal to become an Olympic gold medal-winning diver, then I might want to rethink that. Just a little bit of research would reveal that the number of inexperienced people older than 50 who began a diving career, trained, and won a gold medal at the Olympics would probably be, ohhh, *ZERO*.

I'm not cut out to be an Olympic gold medal-winning diver, some people are not cut out to be rocket scientists, others are horrible at math, some others hate anything that requires salesmanship, and so on.

Here are some things to consider when it comes to setting goals that inspire confidence:

- As mentioned, do your *due diligence. Vet* the project. Do some *research and networking* to get a complete understanding of what needs to be done to achieve your goal.

- Achieving goals is supposed to be fun, and it's not enjoyable to toil away at something that doesn't match your skill set. If you make sure that you're enjoying yourself along the way, it's likely that you're on a potentially successful path.

- Don't go it alone. Get mentoring, link up with partners, and accept support from those around you.

- Don't try to do it all at once. Do it in steps, in increments.

- Do it for fun instead of glory or profit. I may not be able to win an Olympic gold medal, but even though I'm older than 50, I could still take diving lessons and enjoy the sport. Achieving goals for personal satisfaction alone can be a very gratifying part of life.

- After you've done your research, give it a good try. If it leads to a dead-end failure, then at least you won't go to the nursing home wondering what it would have been like if only you'd had the courage to try. Also, as you enthusiastically and actively pursue your unattainable goal, you're more likely to bump into an alternative option than if you'd remained inactive, sitting on the sidelines, eating potato chips and watching TV on the couch. Get up...*go for it!* Good things will happen when you get active and fully engage, even if the end goal turns out to be very different than the one you originally imagined.

Now, make that final plea to your Jury...
Feel this story's truth. Clear your mind, and breathe deeply. Now ask yourself: *What kind of person do I intend to be right now? What do I need to do to feel proud of myself when I'm done?*

Continue breathing deeply — Make a decision — Act!

Back to **Boosting confidence** (page 165)

Let the dog run, or make it heel

After visiting my cousin who lives in Maine, I fell in love with their two Basenji dogs. Basenjis are a breed from Africa; they're the pointy-eared, curly-tailed dogs depicted in hieroglyphics found on pyramid walls.

They don't bark; they have a howl-whine that's called *a yodel.* They have hair, not fur. Finally, they have dispositions that are closer to cats rather than dogs, which can make them a challenge to train. When my cousin summarizes what it's like to own these dogs, he says that Basenjis are "advanced dog ownership."

Packs of Basenjis are still used today to track lions in Africa, to rustle them out of the brush. As an example of their bravery, my cousin's dogs in Maine chased a bear into the woods. He said that he expected to pick up their bones the next day, but they came trotting home unscathed after a few hours.

When I purchased my dogs and told the breeders that I lived in a city, they advised me never to let them off leash. Because they can be as willful as cats, they may not come home when you call them. So when I walk the dogs here in Baltimore, they're always on leash.

Several times in recent years, I've taken the dogs to visit my sister-in-law on her farm in North Carolina. There, with many acres to roam, we figured that it was safe to let them off leash. It was *a joy* to watch them run full stride, weaving among the blueberry bushes, circling the pond, and even sticking half

174

their bodies into holes by the waterside, tracking a possum or some other varmint.

So when it comes to letting the dogs run or putting them on  leash, it depends on the context. In rural Maine or on a large farm in North Carolina, let the dogs run. In the city streets of Baltimore, put the leashes on and get them to heel.

*   *   *

It's often the case that when you identify a negative trait in someone, it's linked to a very positive trait. Think of them as being flip sides of the same coin.

For example, as a younger man, I did a significant amount of work to be a nonjudgmental person. Although I made progress, I noticed several things. First, I never completely stopped being critical; I became a judgmental person who learned how to use compassion to temper my reactions. Second, being judgmental—or "paying attention to detail" — really paid off when I did my writing and editing work.

I often help clients to see both the positive and negative aspects to any character trait. I say to them that it's not a matter of *eliminating* a trait, it's more a matter of *managing* it.

When your personality trait is working well and producing good results, then let the dog run free. When your personality trait is about to make a big mess or stop you from getting what you want, then put a leash on the dog and make him heel.

Now, make that final plea to your Jury...

Feel this story's truth. Clear your mind, and breathe deeply. Now ask yourself: *What kind of person do I intend to be right now? What do I need to do to feel proud of myself when I'm done?*

Continue breathing deeply — Make a decision — Act!

*Back to **Boosting confidence** (page 165)*

Practices should be harder than the games

Since the late 1990s, I've been a *big* fan of the University of Connecticut women's basketball team. My mom's a Connecticut resident, and she and I bond around our love for the team's beautiful, flowing brand of basketball. Before their games were available on the Internet, my mom used to videotape and snail-mail them to me.

The program has won *a ridiculous* 11 national championships (at the time of this writing), including winning four in a row and having completed a handful of undefeated seasons. All of this success and mystique have led to the inevitable question: *why are they so good?* There are a number of noteworthy programs in women's collegiate basketball— Notre Dame, Tennessee, Stanford, Baylor—but what's UConn's *secret sauce?*

Well, after listening to interviews with many former and current players, including superstars such as Sue Bird and Maya Moore, one frequently expressed point stands out. Everyone says that the practices are much, *MUCH* harder than the games. *No contest.*

Let me share some examples. In one drill, the coach asks four of his young women to play a game against five of the male practice players, and it's expected that the women find a way to win. During another drill, players must sprint from one sideline to the other and back, and they have to complete the drill in a certain amount of time. The coaching staff then shortens the time limit and repeats the drill. This continues on and on—with fatigue setting in and the time limits shrinking—until only one player remains standing. Diana Taurasi once said about this drill, *It's not about skill. It's about competitiveness and willing yourself to keep going when your body wants to stop.*

As a less Draconian example, Coach Auriemma and his staff once took his team to see a Broadway production of *The Producers*, and they were able to go backstage to meet stars Matthew Broderick and Nathan Lane. The coaches asked the actors to share their secrets about how they were able to keep their performances top-notch and fresh, even though they had to perform every day for more than a year, and twice on days with matinees. (Their answer? Professionals find a way, no excuses.)

*   *   *

Think about the success of the UConn program in terms of *habits*. That program demands that you get into the habit of showing up every single day and giving it your all. When everything is on the line at the end of the big game, you'll be confident that you've already faced situations five times as difficult in practice. Players have said, *Two minutes left in the game and you're down by 10 points? We do that drill in practice* ***all the time****.*

Confident, successful people don't skate though their day-to-day routines and then "turn it on" for the big interview, speech, or presentation. They maintain daily habits of working hard, and using trial and error to work out the kinks in private. After all the challenging rehearsal, it's only natural that they'll feel confident when those big moments arrive.

Success isn't just a result. It's a daily habit.

Now, make that final plea to your Jury...
Feel this story's truth. Clear your mind, and breathe deeply. Now ask yourself: *What kind of person do I intend to be right now? What do I need to do to feel proud of myself when I'm done?*

Continue breathing deeply — Make a decision — Act!

*Back to **Boosting confidence** (page 165)*

Time travel conversation about driving

Defense Attorney's story for your Jury...

Pretend that we're going to enter a time machine and visit yourself a few years before you learned how to drive a car. (If you've never mastered driving, replace this story with another complex, adult skill set that you've conquered, such as paying taxes, buying a house, completing a college degree, planning and taking a vacation, and so on.)

OK, we've arrived in the past, and you're seeing yourself at 12 or 13 years of age. Imagine that we ask your younger self how she or he feels about driving a car. We might hear a variety of nervous concerns. Maybe the youngster's afraid that that it's not yet legal to be driving. Or maybe the child's worried about getting into an accident, either costing the parents a large sum of money in repairs or being grounded forever for the mishap. We might hear some concern about reaching the pedals, or maybe parts of the dashboard are confusing. It would be quite common to hear worries about fast highway driving.

All in all, I think it's fair to say that this teenager *lacks confidence*, that the person's concerned about what it will take to become a licensed, experienced, safe driver.

So, the first thing that your older self can do is to provide reassurance. Tell this young person who you are, point out that you're living proof of eventual success, and invite the youngster to be at peace with it all. *I'm here to report from the future. There's no doubt. You'll eventually succeed, so you can put aside all your fears and concerns. Relax!*

Take your younger self for a drive, and show the skill you've developed over the years.

Next, it would help to give this young person a sense of how it will all play out. For example, it might be reassuring to know that learning takes place in increments, step by step over time. No one learns how to do everything needed to become an expert driver all at once. A parent might take you to a deserted, huge parking lot so you have plenty of room to practice without doing any damage. An experienced driver can explain the dashboard. Your parents might pay for lessons, so a driving teacher with her own brake pedal will be sitting right beside you as you learn to drive safe, quiet side streets. Eventually, the driving teacher will take your younger self onto the highway at a low-traffic time, and will teach you how to merge safely into highway traffic.

One thing's for sure. After hearing how you did it successfully, the young person begins to feel confident...at least confident enough to begin the process.

Our job in the past is now complete, and we can re-enter the time machine and return to the present day.

*   *   *

Of course, this story is absurd; we can't travel through time. Still, how many times are we intimidated by a complicated task only to end up on the other side of it later, wondering why we were so nervous at the beginning? You prepare by researching, learning, and planning. You practice and build skill over time. You elicit guidance and mentoring along the way. You team with others as needed. You solve problems, often by trial and error. Eventually, *you succeed!*

You've tackled complex projects like this before; you'll do it again.

The next time you face a challenging project and you find your confidence dipping, imagine your future-self coming back in time to reassure you. As you imagine this chat with your future-self, relax and feel confident that it's only a matter of time and effort before you succeed. Just concentrate on taking the initial few steps, and leave the rest for another day.

Finally, if you prefer a technique that involves less imagination and more reality, then use informational interviewing and networking. Find *someone else* who has completed the task you are looking to accomplish, sit down for a half hour over coffee, pick that person's brain, and get some tips that will help you feel confident about completing the task successfully.

Now, make that final plea to your Jury...
Feel this story's truth. Clear your mind, and breathe deeply. Now ask yourself: *What kind of person do I intend to be right now? What do I need to do to feel proud of myself when I'm done?*

Continue breathing deeply — Make a decision — Act!

*Back to **Boosting confidence** (page 165)*

Calming anxiety and fear

Pivot away from irrational anxiety and fear, and into calm.

If you encounter a mugger who pulls a knife on you, see a tractor trailer crossing into your lane and moving toward your car, or spot a rattlesnake on the hiking trail, then that's *rational fear*. Let your fight-or flight response do its thing, and get to safety. *Irrational fear* occurs when *you know* you're safe at the moment, yet you can't shake off your fear.

When experiencing irrational fear about something that isn't happening right at the moment, then use one of these Pivot Inspirations to turn down the crippling feeling of intense fear.

Pivot Inspirations:

- *Don't push it away* (page 184)

- *False alarm* (page 186)

- *It's like riding a bike* (page 189)

- *Just feel the fear* (page 192)

- *Put down that pint of ice cream* (page 194)

- *Stop feeding it attention* (page 197)

- *Turn and face the dog chasing you* (page 200)

Don't push it away

Imagine that you've got yourself a nice, comfortable waterbed. It's served you well for years, giving you many nights of restful sleep. It's one of your valued possessions.

Of course, one of the *worst things* that can happen to a large house-bound container of water is for it to spring a leak. Imagine that you hop onto your treasured waterbed, and a thin, arching spout of water shoots out somewhere on the bed. *Oh, ohhh!*

Now clearly, immediate action is necessary, otherwise the leak will ruin the carpet and the floor. The quickest and most immediate action is to leap toward the leak, and press your hand down hard on the small hole.

On the one hand, no more leak. On the other hand, *what are you going to do now?* Let's hope that you have someone else in the house who can assist you. Or perhaps you can place an object over the small leak until you drain the waterbed in preparation for getting the leak properly repaired.

At this point, I'm going to bend the story in an absurd direction, *but stay with me.* I'm going to exaggerate to make a point.

Imagine that your solution is to press down on the leak and to do nothing more. So for hours and days and weeks and months, you're stuck sitting on the bed, pressing down on a leak, preventing the water from shooting out onto the floor.

184

Even though the pressure on the hole is solving one problem, another problem is developing. The pressure on the rest of the waterbed is uneven; it wasn't designed to withstand this treatment. Eventually, the added pressure will expose another weakness in the mattress, and another leak will spring forth.

Even if you have freakishly long arms and the ability to press down on two leaks simultaneously, it's only a matter of time before the pressure imbalance causes another leak to spout. And then another. *And another!*

*   *   *

Pushing down anxiety —*refusing to feel it or deal with it*—is a lot like pushing down on a water-bed leak. It can give you some temporary relief, but you eventually have to fix the problem or it will pop right back up on you, and it'll be bigger, nastier than before.

Instead, face the scary situation, deal with it, and be done with it.

Now, make that final plea to your Jury...
Feel this story's truth. Clear your mind, and breathe deeply. Now ask yourself: *What kind of person do I intend to be right now? What do I need to do to feel proud of myself when I'm done?*

Continue breathing deeply — Make a decision — Act!

*Back to **Calming anxiety and fear** (page 183)*

False alarm

Imagine that you're a young child in an elementary-school classroom, and suddenly the fire alarm goes off. It's loud, jarring, perhaps a little bit upsetting at first.

The teacher may sigh and wearily direct students to the exits. There may be groans of exasperation, giggling, and even joyful chatter. However, you all dutifully get up, leave the classroom, exit the school, and line up in your class' designated area far from the building.

And then you wait.

One thing that's missing is any kind of *seriousness*, which seems odd given the alarm. *Why is that?*

Well, it's because of experience. This has happened *many times before*, and everyone knows the drill. Do the right thing and follow procedure until you're at a safe distance—*just in case*—and then wait for verification: *it's just a false alarm.*

I mean, take a look around you. There's no fire, no smoke. The teachers and administrators are all calm, perhaps looking bored or even smiling and chatting. Other than the alarm, there *aren't any indications* of threat or danger. If there really was an immediate danger, then you'd be able to tell fairly quickly, right?

Eventually, the fire department arrives, and the fire fighters might look irritated or bored. They know that it's most likely a false alarm. However, they stay focused and continue to do their job; they enter the building to investigate. After ten minutes or so, they come back out, board their vehicles, and drive away. Very soon, the teachers and administrators allow you back into the building, and you make your way to your classroom.

Now, imagine that this was one of those times when you reenter the building as the alarm is still sounding. It's clear to everyone there's no fire—*the professionals from the fire department already verified that*—but for some reason, someone's having a difficult time shutting off the alarm. *That happens.*

Because you know the building's been checked, the sound doesn't bother you. I mean, it's still loud, irritating, and distracting, but you find a way to carry on without paying it much attention, right? It's just a minor technicality that needs to be taken care of before school work resumes.

Instead, imagine what it would be like while re-entering the building if one of your classmates took the continuing alarm seriously. Imagine him yelling, panicking, pointing to the exits, trying to convince everyone to get out of the building *NOW!!!* You'd wonder what was *wrong* with this dude. I mean, he's being foolish by hyper-focusing on one detail while ignoring all evidence of safety. As soon as the administrators do manage to turn off the alarm, that person's is going to look very silly.

Thankfully, it wasn't you acting that way, right?

*   *   *

On the one hand, you feel what you feel, and that's always true, valid, and OK. On the other hand, what feels true can be flat-out wrong.

When people have been hurt badly or often, they develop a hypersensitive reaction to certain situations (we call these *triggers*). For example, we may feel intensely fearful of a threat even though logic tells us that we're completely safe.

When facing a strong feeling that doesn't match reality, consider it to be a false alarm. Your wiring got crossed. Check to make sure there's no threat, breathe deeply, reassure yourself, and then go back and face that situation even though your emotional alarm continues to sound. It'll be turned off in a short while, as soon as reengaging with normal activities makes you *feel* as safe as you *truly are.*

Now, make that final plea to your Jury...

Feel this story's truth. Clear your mind, and breathe deeply. Now ask yourself: *What kind of person do I intend to be right now? What do I need to do to feel proud of myself when I'm done?*

Continue breathing deeply — Make a decision — Act!

Back to **Calming anxiety and fear** (page 183)

It's like riding a bike

Defense Attorney's story for your Jury...
When facing a scary situation, we often hyper-focus on a difficulty, such as the idea that something bad might happen or that we might get hurt. Let's make sure we don't lose sight of the very low probability of serious harm, and how deliriously *happy* we'll be once we overcome challenges and succeed.

As a great example, remember the freedom, exhilaration, and fun of riding a bicycle. I mentioned this to a client recently, and he beamed brightly and bounced in his chair, sharing some of the great times he had while biking with his boyhood friends. (If you've never learned to ride a bicycle, remember instead another fun childhood activity that required some risk at the beginning, such as learning to roller skate, earning a spot on a sports team or cheerleading squad,  learning to cook, or learning to use tools.)

Now, just about everyone falls—or otherwise suffers some scrapes and bruises—while learning to ride a bike. I have a distinct memory of losing control on a narrow sidewalk and running into a bush. Even so, there was no way that those minor setbacks were going to keep us from learning how to ride. Perhaps we were striving to keep up with an older brother or sister. Maybe we wanted to accompany friends who'd already learned to ride. Or maybe we saw the movie *E.T.: The Extra-Terrestrial* one too many times and just had to experience bike riding.

Remember that your parents made sure you didn't disregard safety altogether. Those of you who are younger may have had knee pads and helmets. I know I used training wheels for a while to help me with balance at the very beginning, and I remember my dad running alongside the bike as I pedaled. It wasn't long before we were past the point of frequent stops, starts, and falls, and we were free, riding like the wind.

*   *   *

Some of the best parts of life require some effort and pain. Very few of us found the love of our lives without first having our hearts broken at least once. We may have undergone some painful experiences at work—including possible demotion, embarrassment, or firing—before we found our niche elsewhere, got a second wind, or found a mentor to guide us past the landmines.

The next time you face a challenging task whose completion excites and motivates you, remind yourself that it's like riding a bike. At first, it's intimidating. You may need to prepare or find ways to limit any potential hurt. There will be fits and starts, short-term setbacks, and perhaps some "skinned knees." Regardless, you'll make it to the other side, and you'll be *so glad when you do.*

In the same way you approached riding a bike, don't let the potential for short term, minor pain steal from you some of the greatest pleasures in life. Remind yourself that it will all be *so worthwhile in the end!*

Now, make that final plea to your Jury...
Feel this story's truth. Clear your mind, and breathe deeply. Now ask yourself: *What kind of person do I intend to be right now? What do I need to do to feel proud of myself when I'm done?*

Continue breathing deeply — Make a decision — Act!

*Back to **Calming anxiety and fear** (page 183)*

Just feel the fear

Imagine standing in a field, and the wind picks up. Feel it blow against your face, your clothing.

Now, we all know we can't push the wind away, prevent it from blowing against us. It's equally absurd to think we can open our arms wide, encircle them around the breeze, and somehow capture the wind.

You are.

The wind is.

You feel it.

The wind doesn't "mean" anything. You don't have to *do* anything with it. You don't have to *react* in any particular way. Simply notice the experience of feeling the wind. *Just feel it*, and let that be enough for now.

In time, the wind dies down after the weather changes, and you move on to your next experience.

*   *   *

Imagine now that you react to *your difficult emotions* the same way you experience the wind. In particular, imagine feeling fear that way, especially *irrational fear*.

192

Fear comes up like the wind, you can feel the experience of it on your body just as you might a gust of wind, and it subsides in time, just as the wind does.

Understand that your irrational fear doesn't "mean" anything. You don't have to *do* anything with it. You don't have to *react* to your fear in any particular way. Simply notice the experience of feeling fear. *Just feel it*, and let that be enough for now.

In time, the fear dies down as you move on with your life, just as it does after a blustery day when milder weather finally returns.

Now, make that final plea to your Jury...
Feel this story's truth. Clear your mind, and breathe deeply. Now ask yourself: *What kind of person do I intend to be right now? What do I need to do to feel proud of myself when I'm done?*

Continue breathing deeply — Make a decision — Act!

Back to **Calming anxiety and fear** (page 183)

Put down that pint of ice cream

Defense Attorney's story for your Jury...

I recently started working with a client who was adjusting to a new senior management position. She'd been jumping in to do her subordinates' work instead of delegating: *It would just be quicker and easier for me to do it myself.* She also had been working an unreasonable number of hours.

At first, our work focused on coaching her direct reports to perform, and on setting limits and boundaries. Yet, there was an unspoken concern slowing everything down, a nagging worry that something might go terribly wrong unless she grabbed control of every situation.

So, our focus shifted from management techniques to addressing her anxiety and tolerating risk. After sharing with me that she also engaged in compulsive cleaning binges at home, she remarked, *My family jokes that it's impossible to pry the bottle of Windex from my hand!*

To put things into perspective, I asked her to reflect on times

when she'd gone through a very difficult disappointment or loss, or when she'd had a particularly rough week. When that happens, it's normal to curl up on the couch sometimes, wrap yourself in a blanket, plunge a spoon into a pint of fancy ice cream, and disappear into a favorite movie.

194

Micro-managing at work and compulsive cleaning at home were her "pint of ice cream."

She asked, *Is it OK to do that?*

Sure, *for one night!* However, just notice how ugly it can get if it turns into two, four, or 15 nights in a row. It's important to have more tools in your tool belt than "eat a pint of ice cream when I feel bad." We all need other ways to soothe ourselves. Better yet, it would help tremendously if we also had tools we could use to reduce the underlying causes of the anxiety.

In the same way that we all have to put down the pint of ice cream after a one-night binge, my client needs to put down the Windex and the micromanaging.

*   *   *

We humans have a limitless number of activities we can use to take the edge off of anxiety: eating, shopping, self-medicating with drugs and alcohol, hoarding, cleaning, and superstitious rituals.

The problem is that *they work!* They soothe you, and you give a hit of relief. The *bigger* problem is that the relief doesn't last long, causing you to chase it by doing your soothing ritual again. Do it often enough, and it takes on the look-and-feel of an addiction.

Other Pivot Inspirations present methods for dealing with anxiety head on. This story is about reminding yourself not to over rely on a temporary solution. When you find yourself grabbing at something easy and holding on a bit too long, ask yourself to "put down that pint of ice cream."

Now, make that final plea to your Jury...

Feel this story's truth. Clear your mind, and breathe deeply. Now ask yourself: *What kind of person do I intend to be right now? What do I need to do to feel proud of myself when I'm done?*

Continue breathing deeply — Make a decision — Act!

Back to **Calming anxiety and fear** (page 183)

Stop feeding it attention

Consider a campfire. They're fun! You can use them for heat, cooking your food, and a great place to keep company with friends and loved ones.

As useful as a campfire can be, there comes a time when you want the fire to go out. You could use water to douse it. As another option, you could throw dirt onto it and stir it. I suppose you could use a fire extinguisher on it, but no one actually does that with a campfire.

I remember at the end of my Boy Scout camping trips, on the morning before we were due to pack our belongings and leave the site, we'd use another method for putting out the fire: we'd just stop feeding it.

No more kindling, no more sticks, and no more logs. No more blowing on it to stoke flames. And certainly keep the lighter fluid away from it.

After a few hours, take a stick and spread out the glowing embers so more of them are exposed to air. Then...*just leave it alone!* The fire has only so much fuel, and it will run out eventually. As long as it's secure in a pit with cleared brush all around it and water buckets at the ready, just let it burn itself out.

Irrational fear can be very much like a large campfire that would be difficult to douse with water or dirt. It's best to let it die down a bit on its own, first.

So, to *stop putting twigs and kindling on the Fear Fire*, you can remove some physical tension from your body. To accomplish that goal, clear your mind, relax your face into a slight smile, stretch, and breathe deeply. These physical adjustments send signals to your body that it's OK to relax.

Stop putting logs onto it by removing your attention from it. Distract yourself with another compelling activity that holds your attention, soothe yourself with a hot shower or a tasty snack or some other sensually pleasing activity, and practice patience.

Stop throwing gasoline or lighter fluid on it by imagining "the worst that could possibly happen," or by letting your fearful thoughts speed up, bombarding you with images and thoughts of possible pain and suffering. Instead, remind yourself that it's OK to feel afraid, but that doesn't necessarily mean that there's anything serious to fear. You don't have to dwell or act on it. Then, refocus and get busy with an engaging activity that's unrelated to your fear.

The more you divert your attention and immerse yourself in some unrelated task, the less fuel there is for your Fear Fire. Starved of Attention Fuel, the fire will soon be small enough to take care of with a small amount of water, a little dirt, some stirring, and a few crunching stomps of your boot.

Now, make that final plea to your Jury...
Feel this story's truth. Clear your mind, and breathe deeply. Now ask yourself: *What kind of person do I intend to be right now? What do I need to do to feel proud of myself when I'm done?*

Continue breathing deeply — Make a decision — Act!

*Back to **Calming anxiety and fear** (page 183)*

Turn and face the dog chasing you

Defense Attorney's story for your Jury...

I can vividly recall a time, as a very small boy, when I encountered an unfamiliar German Shepard dog while playing in a ball field.

I eyed him. He eyed me right back...intently.

Oh, no. This isn't good!

I knew I couldn't *outfight him*, but I thought I might be able to *outrun him*. He was some distance away from me, after all.

So, I spun on my heels and bolted toward home. To my surprise and horror, I'd gone only a few strides before I heard the dog bearing down on me from behind, breathing heavily and pounding sod with his big paws. I sprinted faster, but it was no use. The dog was going to catch me.

In that moment, I signaled my surrender with a dead stop.

What happened next surprised me. Instead of pouncing on me and using me as a dog chew, he circled to the front, did a Downward Facing Dog pose by lowering head and raising his butt; he then wagged his tail playfully, barked, circled back behind me, and then ran away.

Other childhood experiences with dogs were similar. When I ran, the dog chased me. When I ran faster, he matched and surpassed my speed. The minute I stopped running, the dog knew that the game was over, got bored, and trotted away.

When facing a true threat, it's very helpful when fear ignites your fight-or-flight response. If you're facing a mugger with a knife or if you notice your car drifting toward a tractor trailer in the next lane on the highway, *please DO get away* from the imminent danger. Fighting or fleeing is *most appropriate*.

If you're facing an *irrational fear*, one that you want to reduce in your life, I often think that it behaves like a dog chasing a child. The more you run, the more energized, scary, and threatening your fear becomes. If you stop running—perhaps even courageously turn to face the fear—it knows that the jig is up and it goes away. Maybe not instantly, but it's then only a matter of time before it disengages and wanders away.

Now, make that final plea to your Jury...
Feel this story's truth. Clear your mind, and breathe deeply. Now ask yourself: *What kind of person do I intend to be right now? What do I need to do to feel proud of myself when I'm done?*

Continue breathing deeply — Make a decision — Act!

*Back to **Calming anxiety and fear** (page 183)*

Changing unhelpful beliefs

Pivot away from stubbornness and into a willingness to try something new.

Pivot Inspirations:

- *Burning your hand on the stove* (page 204)

- *"Maybe, we'll see!"* (page 208)

- *Renegotiating the contract* (page 210)

- *Wear the boxer down with jabs* (page 212)

- *Whose family did you think you were dealing with?* (page 215)

Burning your hand on the stove

Defense Attorney's story for your Jury...

Imagine that mom's busy cooking dinner, and she doesn't see her four-year-old daughter enter the kitchen, approaching the stove. Being a typically curious child, the little girl reaches toward the cooking food, touches the hot pan, and cries out in pain. *Ouch!*

Mom pulls the little girl aside, tends to her burn, gives her a hug, and wipes away her tears. Then, she imparts some wisdom designed to protect her child from harm. She says firmly, *Stay away from the stove...it's dangerous!* This really *makes an impression* on the child given the aching pain and her mother's impassioned, concerned plea.

She decides that the warning **Stay away from the stove...it's dangerous!** is literally fixed and true, and that she'll strictly obey the new rule. This is a very practical approach for a four-year-old child; no one would argue with it. Though, as children mature and age, they normally adapt rules like this, modifying them for more adult activity and accomplishment, right? The safety rules of a four-year-old wouldn't apply to a 25-year-old.

That being said, let me play out this story in an extreme way just to illustrate a point. In this case, let's say that the little girl was so shaken that she applied this rule with extreme seriousness and rigidity, never questioning it, never changing it in any way over time.

Imagine a few years later. Her father has prepared a meal, calls out to his daughter to come to the stove, and asks her to carry a plate of food to the table. She looks at him wide-eyed, cries, and steps back away from the stove, refusing to carry the plate. *Stay away from the stove...it's dangerous!*

The daughter's now 10 years old and can't boil water or cook an egg at the stove. *Stay away from the stove...it's dangerous!*

She's 15, and seeing her friends cook macaroni and cheese on the stove causes her to run out of the kitchen screaming. *Stay away from the stove...it's dangerous!*

She's now an adult, is unable to cook for herself, never throws dinner parties, seems odd to other adults, and yet continues to apply the rule rigidly. *Stay away from the stove...it's dangerous!*

Obviously, this would never happen. *Stay away from the stove...it's dangerous!* is the best way to protect a four-year-old, but it needs to be updated so it's more appropriate for adults. Here's an example of a reasonable update to the rule: *The stove is a very useful tool, but you can burn yourself if you're not careful; be sure to use pan handles, proper utensils, and pot holders.*

As mentioned, this is an absurd example. However, it begs the question, how many other decisions did we make as children that remain unmodified and that deeply restrict our lives to this day?

When we were children, we did the very best we could to understand ourselves and our world. Along the way, there were various painful experiences, both big and small, and we did the very best we could to protect ourselves, to prevent being hurt again.

In most cases, we did a very good job, and we expanded our understanding of life over time. In some instances, though, our assessments became stuck, and we're still living according to the well-intentioned but very flawed, limiting assessments of a child. We might still be operating out of beliefs such as these that have outlived their usefulness:

I'm ugly.

The world is a scary and dangerous place.

I'm unlovable.

Everybody lies and cheats.

It's mean to say no to others.

Whoever has the most toys when she dies, wins.

I need to be perfect.

I have to do it; otherwise, it won't get done.

It's wrong to hurt other people's feelings, and that must be avoided at all costs.

When you're facing a very strong belief that's limiting your ability to thrive, ask yourself how you can modify it so you can move forward in the same way that "be careful and use proper utensils" allowed the woman in the story to use the stove safely.

Now, make that final plea to your Jury...

Feel this story's truth. Clear your mind, and breathe deeply. Now ask yourself: *What kind of person do I intend to be right now? What do I need to do to feel proud of myself when I'm done?*

Continue breathing deeply — Make a decision — Act!

*Back to **Changing unhelpful beliefs** (page 203)*

"Maybe, we'll see!"

On the one hand, beliefs are very powerful in the way they motivate you, reassure you, or provide some peace of mind. On the other hand, if we believe something strongly enough, then it shuts the door to learning anything new. For example, if we have a dysfunctional belief, we often get stuck with it, because it's buffered itself from feedback of any kind, including the truth.

History is filled with examples of things that we once believed that turned out to be untrue. The earth didn't turn out to be flat, even though many believed it to be so. The sun, moon, and stars don't revolve around the earth, and the earth isn't the center of the universe. Even research-backed beliefs sometimes fail us; ten years ago or so, we briefly believed that orally taking mega doses of Vitamin E was healthy (nope...it's actually *harmful*).

So, when a stubborn-yet-unhelpful belief stands in our way, what can we do?

A great first step is to *decide not to be so sure*. Leave the door open a crack to the idea that there might be more to the story, that there might be more to learn, or even that you could be entirely, horribly wrong.

The next time you're feeling compelled by a strong belief that you know has been causing you problems, have a chat with that belief. Say to yourself, *You may be right about that, but let's save the discussion for later. Let me go off and try something new and see how that works out. When I'm finished, I promise that we can discuss it again.* (If you have a God-centered religious practice, then consider using the phrase: *let go, and let God.* Don't let your beliefs bully you into avoiding action. Give God a little bit more wiggle room to impart grace and insight to you.)

In this way, you're showing respect for your old belief by not dismissing it completely. At the same time, you're not allowing your belief to prevent you from taking action, which could give you some new information needed to modify or change that unhelpful belief.

I don't know. Maybe! We'll see.

Now, make that final plea to your Jury...
Feel this story's truth. Clear your mind, and breathe deeply. Now ask yourself: *What kind of person do I intend to be right now? What do I need to do to feel proud of myself when I'm done?*

Continue breathing deeply — Make a decision — Act!

Back to **Changing unhelpful beliefs** (page 203)

Renegotiating the contract

When facing an unhelpful belief, the most challenging task is getting past your own iron clad certainty. I mean, why rethink something if you believe with your whole heart and soul that you're right?

When sensing that you're being unreasonably stubborn about protecting a belief, remind yourself that beliefs are like legal contracts.

For example, legal contracts are very serious. If you violate a contract, you're vulnerable to being sued. So, it's important to craft contracts with care, and to heed the contract carefully after it's been signed.

That being said, contracts can be renegotiated and rewritten. It happens all the time. In many cases, a contract has an expiration date, at which point the parties can renew it, renegotiate it, or terminate it.

Just like solidly constructed contracts, your personal beliefs should be reviewed periodically. Remind yourself that you're more experienced and more knowledgeable now than when you first formed that belief. (For example, musicians for decades have complained that their initial record contracts took advantage of their lack of experience. In future contracts, the musicians were smarter about being paid fairly.) Also, the world keeps on changing, so there may be circumstances that have developed that didn't exist when you decided what's what.

(For example, marketplace rents change over time, so you don't want a lease that goes on for too many years before it's adjusted for current prices.)

Be very open to reviewing your beliefs regularly. You will often find that tweaking, seriously modifying, or terminating your belief can *greatly*, **greatly** benefit you in the same way reviewing legal contracts can be in your own best interest.

Now, make that final plea to your Jury...
Feel this story's truth. Clear your mind, and breathe deeply. Now ask yourself: *What kind of person do I intend to be right now? What do I need to do to feel proud of myself when I'm done?*

Continue breathing deeply — Make a decision — Act!

Back to **Changing unhelpful beliefs** (page 203)

Wear the boxer down with jabs

Defense Attorney's story for your Jury...
Let's say you have a dysfunctional, unhelpful belief, and you've decided it needs to go, but getting rid of it feels intimidating. Here's a game you can play that could lighten up your approach and make it more manageable.

Pretend that you're in the boxing ring with your belief, and it becomes very clear at the beginning of the bout that you're not going to score a knockout—get rid of the belief or change it—with one, quick punch. It's too skilled to leave itself open like that. Instead, you're going to have to wear it down with jabs.

For example, you might practice keeping an open mind and being on the lookout for evidence that contradicts your belief. [*smack...thwap, thwap*] Try to poke holes in some of its key arguments. [*thwap, thwap, thwap*] Look for contradictions! [*thwap*] Point out examples of how following this belief causes major grief in your life. [*thwap, thwap...smack!*] Try something different, and point out to your belief how much better things turned out. [*thwap, thwap...thwap, thwap*]

You may recall the Muhammad Ali strategy used against George Foreman called *rope-a-dope*. Your belief might be too strong to fight in the beginning, and you may need to take a few punches and ride the ropes until it tires itself out a bit. Then, it's time to wear it down with jabs. Just avoid getting knocked out until you can get in your punches later in the bout.

If you execute this plan well, one of two things will happen. Either you'll wear the belief down to the point where a knockout punch is possible. Or you'll win the match in a decision. Be patient, do bits of damage when you get an easy opening, and wait for your opportunity to win. Think like Muhammad Ali: *it's just a matter of time!*

*   *   *

For many people, struggling against dysfunctional beliefs— *I'm a loser, I'm not good enough, I'm unlovable, I can never win, or the system's rigged*—can feel like a battle. Your mind tells you that the belief is flawed, but you fear deep down that it's true. Using this imagination exercise brings the battle right to the forefront.

Are you feeling kind of beat up? Tired of it? Feeling aggressive in response? Then hop into the ring!

As another way to look at this story, it's all in the imagination. In a sense, it's a game. Any time you can use a game, humor, or fun in the way you approach a personal struggle, the more you'll be able to tap into curiosity and creativity needed to succeed.

So, *play with it.* Don't take it all *so seriously.* (It's only life, after all.) Use your imagination and engage in a sports fantasy. I don't know about you, but in all my sports fantasies, I always end up winning.

Now, make that final plea to your Jury...

Feel this story's truth. Clear your mind, and breathe deeply. Now ask yourself: *What kind of person do I intend to be right now? What do I need to do to feel proud of myself when I'm done?*

Continue breathing deeply — Make a decision — Act!

*Back to **Changing unhelpful beliefs** (page 203)*

Whose family did you think you were dealing with?

Defense Attorney's story for your Jury...
After an upsetting experience involving my mother, I decided to unload on my Life & Career Coach during our meeting the following week. I was hoping to get some validation about how unreasonable she'd been and to generate a bit of sympathy. Being a good sport, he gave me the go ahead to begin my story.

My graduation ceremony had been that past weekend. I'd received my master's degree in Clinical Social Work on Sunday afternoon.

My mother and aunt—both retired and in their mid-sixties—decided they wanted to drive to Boston to be there for me. They'd arrive on Saturday, spend the night at a hotel, attend the ceremony early Sunday afternoon, and drive back home later that day.

Hearing this, I immediately thought "make a reservation at a nice, quiet place, and have a pleasant meal with my mom and my aunt." *Perfect!* I could do some research ahead of time to find a place with a menu acceptable to my mom; her tastes lie squarely within the safe realm of mainstream American cuisine. The idea seemed so...*reasonable*, and I suggested it to my mother.

But she had other ideas.

*Oh, Let's go to Faneuil Hall and Quincy Market. I **love** that place!*, she said.

On the one hand, my gut was telling me that that was not a great idea. On the other hand, reverting back to The Good Son Who Wants to Please His Mother, I said yes.

As brief background, Faneuil Hall and Quincy Market is a major Boston tourist area; it draws more people annually than Disney World. The walkway around the market is made of old cobblestone, which is not a friendly surface for two people about to enter their Golden Years. Also, the area tended more toward bars and fast food than quieter, more civilized dining. Finally, the hotel where my mom and aunt were staying was nowhere close, creating a logistical challenge. Still...we could make it work.

So on Saturday night, we arrived at the marketplace, explored the main buildings, and did the touristy-shopping thing for a while. Eventually, it was time to eat.

We rejected one place, because there was a band playing loud music. Continuing our circling and growing a bit weary from the walking, we finally found a sit-down restaurant with cloth covered tables, a reasonably quiet atmosphere, and a middle-of-the-road American-food menu that would meet with my mom's approval. I checked the menu and wait time (20 minutes), I got approval from my mom and aunt, and I went back to the hostess to put my name on the list.

When I returned, I noticed my aunt standing alone outside the restaurant wearing a bemused smile on her face. I asked,

Where's mom? She said, *Gerry, **I don't know**. She just took off down there.* I glanced down the walkway and noticed my mom meandering among the shops. My aunt and I just shrugged and hustled to catch up with her. When we asked her if she'd changed her mind about the restaurant, all she'd say was, *Let's just **wander** awhile.*

Okaaay!

Completing one more circuit of the marketplace, our feet really beginning to bark, we passed the bar where the band had been playing earlier, and my mom said, *Oh, why don't we just eat HERE!* Tired, hungry, and not in the mood to resist, my aunt and I agreed.

Well, it was for the most part just a bar. The tables weren't very clean, and the food was mediocre deli food. As you might have guessed by now, the band was merely on break. Half way through our sandwiches, the music resumed, making it almost impossible to carry on any kind of conversation.

I wasn't pleased while it was happening (though I kept my complaints to myself), and I was now venting my displeasure to my Life & Career Coach.

*What's so hard about making a **dinner** reservation? I would have been MORE than happy to have set that up ahead of time. Why couldn't we have had a nice meal with some decent conversation so I could catch up with my mom and aunt? What was the deal with her rejecting the nicer restaurant we eventually DID find at the marketplace? How did such a simple thing turn out to be such a Cluster [Freak]?* Blah, blah, blah....

My Life & Career Coach was a very patient man, and we'd been working together for a considerable length of time. When I wound down my tale of woe, he smiled and said wryly:

*I don't know whose family **you** thought you were dealing with, but it certainly couldn't have been **yours**....*

Cracking up laughing, I simultaneously wanted to hug him and hit him with a two-by-four. He was *right*, damn it.

To this day, if I notice myself getting irritated when situations don't match my expectations, I mumble, *I don't know whose family YOU thought you were dealing with*, I smile, I relax, and then I find myself more willing to play nicely with the hand I've been dealt.

*   *   *

When I first decided to include this story in the book, I wasn't sure in which category it belonged, because it involves a few different themes. Calming emotions? Acceptance? Managing anger? Enjoying the journey of life?

I finally decided that, at its core, this story is about letting go of beliefs: the belief that I needed to prove to my mom that I was a good son, the belief that there was some "normal" way to have a graduation celebration, or the belief that my mom should have been able to rally for this special occasion instead of behaving exactly as I'd known her to act my entire life. It's about letting go of the "shoulds and shouldn'ts" and playing nicely with "what is."

Once you shift that perspective, the end result is *relief* and an ability to *laugh* about it.

Now, make that final plea to your Jury...
Feel this story's truth. Clear your mind, and breathe deeply. Now ask yourself: *What kind of person do I intend to be right now? What do I need to do to feel proud of myself when I'm done?*

Continue breathing deeply — Make a decision — Act!

Back to **Changing unhelpful beliefs** (page 203)

Competing

Pivot away from dislike of competition and into acceptance of it.

Pivot Inspirations:

- *More fun to keep score* (page 222)

- *Personal best* (page 225)

More fun to keep score

When it comes to online gaming, I'm *older* than Old School. Just about the only game I play is Solitaire.

When I play Solitaire on my tablet, the app keeps track of stats about how well my win did as compared with other games I'd won that month. For example, it tracks how the speed of my card placement compared with other wins.

Recently after winning a game, I looked at the score, and it ranked the win as being number 1 in all categories. I was *thrilled.* Still, I had a sneaking suspicion that the win wasn't all that it appeared to be. So, I looked closely at the statistics, and it told me that this was the best win of the month because it was the *only* win of the month. Bummer!

I tell this story to show that we all can be competitive creatures, at least in the sense that we find it really enjoyable to build our skill, learn something new, and do better than we did before.

I see this most often in the games that we play. Let me use basketball as an example. You can randomly shoot baskets for the heck of it, though most people will quickly grow bored. Before you know it, you'll be measuring distance, seeing if you can hit longer shots. Perhaps you'll count how many times you can hit shots from the free throw line.

Just notice the pattern. Once you've mastered one skill, your mind naturally looks for ways to make things more interesting and challenging. Soon, you'll be playing the game of HORSE with friends. It's only a matter of time before you're playing two-on-two or a full-court game of basketball.

Although winning is fun, it's not the best thing about competition. What really rocks the house is how much fun it is to become more skilled, and it's easier to get better if you keep score in some way. Also, people find that the quickest, best way to improve skill level is to compete against a higher and higher level of competition.

Finally, it's not just sports. You can see this "let's keep score" tendency in sales quotas at work, top 10 lists, award shows, trying to throw a more impressive dinner party than the neighbor, and maintaining your lawn better. Win or lose, notice how much fun it is to strive to do *better*.

*   *   *

The next time you find yourself feeling intimidated or otherwise nervous about a competitive situation, remove your attention from "winning and losing" and place it on "let me try to get better." Try beating your last, best outing. Compete against stronger adversaries so you'll have to try harder, be more creative, and respond more nimbly than if you were competing against people you know you can beat.

I was watching the TV music competition *American Idol* recently, and a contestant really impressed me. He'd made it past the initial audition the previous year, but had gotten knocked out within the next few rounds. At his audition this year, his performance was so strong that the judges didn't debate at all and just held up his ticket to the next round.

Before exiting, he said to the judges, *Can you give me something more? I don't want to just go on to the next round. I want to get better.* Harry Connick, Jr. arched an eyebrow and said, *OK.* Harry then proceeded to give him some highly technical advice about how to work within all of the chords in the song when soloing at the end of the performance. The contestant was attentive and very grateful for the opportunity to learn something new.

As another example, the drummer for the rock band Rush, Neil Peart, recently said that he'd heard an Eric Clapton quote saying that, when he first heard Jimi Hendrix, he wanted to burn his guitar. Neil said, *I don't understand that. When I'm around musicians who are better than I am, it makes me want to go practice some more, so I can do what **they're** doing!*

It's not about winning and losing. It's about the thrill of improvement and hitting heights that would be hard to achieve if you were going it alone.

Now, make that final plea to your Jury...

Feel this story's truth. Clear your mind, and breathe deeply. Now ask yourself: *What kind of person do I intend to be right now? What do I need to do to feel proud of myself when I'm done?*

Continue breathing deeply — Make a decision — Act!

*Back to **Competing** (page 221)*

Personal best

Defense Attorney's story for your Jury...
One year during high school, I ran long-distance races on the track and field team. Although I've never been and never will be a great runner, it was an excellent experience, and I learned a lot.

As with all sports, people would cheer the winners, urging them on to their first-, second-, or third-place finishes. So, being a fairly slow runner in the one-mile and two-mile races, I'd cross the finish line well after the excitement for the winners had settled down.

I remember the first time I discovered that track and field events offered an interesting race-within-a-race that created some fan excitement. There were times when, long after the top runners crossed the finish line, the coaches, other athletes, and the crowd would be cheering energetically for a runner way back in the pack.

Let's go. GO! You can do it. On pace for a PR! ***PR!!!***

"PR" stood for "personal record," sometimes called a "personal best." The coaches had been checking their stopwatches and noticed that, if the runner kept up the current pace or bettered it for the remainder of the run, that person will submit a personal-best time.

Sometimes, the cheering was louder and more enthusiastic for a "loser" who set a PR than for any of the winners.

225

*   *   *

Many people feel that the best thing about competition is that, in the pursuit of victory, *everybody* is striving to become better. While pursuing the best and trying to win the competition, your level of success rises during the chase, your skill level increases, and both you and your team benefit.

In team sports, not everyone can be a star, but a star alone can't win a game. Teams need role players who are willing to do their very best in a limited support role. Also, star athletes may become injured or simply graduate, leaving an open slot for a new star. If you've been concentrating on setting new personal-best records while serving as a role player, you'll be ready to shine like a star, should the opportunity arise.

The next time you're in a competitive situation, make sure that you keep an eye on your personal best, and congratulate yourself when you surpass it. Because we end up turning right around and running another race as soon as we're finished with the last one, it could be argued that improving your PR— self-improvement—should be the only competition that really matters.

In the end, the only race you run is against yourself.

Now, make that final plea to your Jury...

Feel this story's truth. Clear your mind, and breathe deeply. Now ask yourself: *What kind of person do I intend to be right now? What do I need to do to feel proud of myself when I'm done?*

Continue breathing deeply — Make a decision — Act!

Back to **Competing** (page 221)

226

Pivot away from impatience and being driven by results, and into a relaxed, day-to-day appreciation.

Pivot Inspirations:

- *Enjoying the exercise itself* (page 228)

- *Let it ebb and flow naturally* (page 231)

- *Unexpected benefits* (page 233)

- *Winning the tournament* (page 235)

Enjoying the exercise itself

Defense Attorney's story for your Jury...
As mentioned throughout this book, I recently took on a gym routine with the primary goal of losing belly weight. Very early in the process, I bumped into the limitations of goal setting.

For example, in the initial months, after increasing the time and intensity of my work on the elliptical machine, I'd eagerly look forward to my weekly weigh-in on Friday morning. Often, I was disappointed. Either I would have lost no weight, or I'd have lost fewer pounds than expected. This led to second guessing, pushing harder than my body could tolerate, and shifting emphasis from *just fit into your pants better* to *you need to hit **this number**.* In brief summary, it was unpleasant and stressful.

As another example, in an effort to vary my aerobics—you know, shake it up a little bit so that my body wouldn't grow too accustomed to my routine—I began to do brief parts of my workout on the stationary bike and on the treadmill. Now, I'd heard from acquaintances of mine who are Health & Wellness Coaches that jogging was being deemphasized because of the pounding it places on the knees. Still, I found myself getting caught up in wanting to increase the speed and distance slightly every time I ran. *It's just a matter of time before I'll be at a great pace for running the Baltimore Half Marathon!*

No, it was just a matter of time before I pulled a calf muscle and had to take off ten days to heal.

Eventually, I changed my focus from achieving goals as quickly as possible to enjoying myself during my workouts. It became clear that it would be silly for me to kill myself in the gym for six months, lose the weight quickly, and then go back to living an unhealthy lifestyle. In other words, it was going to take *a few years* to achieve my overall goals, so I'd better settle into this gym routine, and make friends with it. I made peace with the idea that I was going to be here for a while.

It was then that I began focusing on enjoying myself as much as I could week to week. I figured out on which days I should lift weights given how long it took this 50-plus-year-old body to recover from soreness and fatigue. I found that *monthly* small adjustments to my speed and distance on the treadmill were much more comfortable. I even hired a personal trainer for the first time ever; he helped me to incorporate the latest and greatest techniques into my routine.

Oh, I still care if I lose weight, and I *am* reaching my goals; I still make it to the gym three to four times a week. It's just that slowing down and focusing on enjoyment are helping me to stay the course much better than stressing myself out and driving myself to hit some arbitrary numbers.

*   *   *

On the one hand, aiming for measurable goals is an important part of achieving results. On the other hand, enjoying yourself is an important part of motivation and assists in helping you to stay committed to a long-term project.

In what other areas of your life are you pushing too hard unnecessarily to get to the finish line? In those instances, how can you lower the stress and focus on making the process more enjoyable? In what ways can you remind yourself that the journey *is at least equally as important* as the destination?

Now, make that final plea to your Jury...

Feel this story's truth. Clear your mind, and breathe deeply. Now ask yourself: *What kind of person do I intend to be right now? What do I need to do to feel proud of myself when I'm done?*

Continue breathing deeply — Make a decision — Act!

Back to **Enjoying the journey of life** (page 227)

Let it ebb and flow naturally

Defense Attorney's story for your Jury...
Early one January, I had my first Life & Career Coaching meeting of the year with a client I'd been seeing for some months. In the weeks leading up to the end-of-the-year holidays, she'd just begun to do some serious professional networking, seeking informational interviews from acquaintances and peers.

After beginning the meeting with some friendly chit-chat, I asked her how she was doing with her goals. She then looked sheepishly at me and said that she accomplished *NOTHING* since we'd last met. I smiled and said *Well, I'll bet you accomplished a lot. If you're like most people, you got some rest, visited or otherwise caught up with family members, took some time off work, relaxed, and enjoyed yourself.*

I followed up by saying that no one stays on point every day, all year long, during a long-term project such as investigating a career change. The intensity level naturally varies over time. I also mentioned that my most successful clients took off a week or two here and there, and that those reasonable breaks didn't affect their success level. The trick was not to let some reasonable time off—a few days, a week or two—turn into months or years.

*   *   *

When working on long-term efforts, it can be helpful to turn to nature for examples of cycles, flow, and movement over time.

231

For example, think of the ebb and flow of the tides. The tide flows in, and the tide flows out. When the tide flows back out, we don't freak out and worry that we'll never, ever get to experience high tide again. We understand that it's a natural cycle, that it's only a matter of time before the water flows back in again.

When you get off track with your personal projects, consider that the tide flowed back out. It's OK, it's natural! You needed a rest, another project temporarily became a higher priority, or some other good reason led to the interruption. As soon as you can, refocus on your goal, take some action, and ride the tide back in.

Now, make that final plea to your Jury...

Feel this story's truth. Clear your mind, and breathe deeply. Now ask yourself: *What kind of person do I intend to be right now? What do I need to do to feel proud of myself when I'm done?*

Continue breathing deeply — Make a decision — Act!

Back to **Enjoying the journey of life** (page 227)

Unexpected benefits

Defense Attorney's story for your Jury...

Time and energy permitting, it can be great to try something different just for the heck of it, even if you aren't sure exactly what you're going to gain. Let me tell you a story to illustrate this point.

A few years ago, I received an invitation to join a networking group. The purpose of this group is for members who meet with each other weekly to exchange qualified referrals for services, and each chapter can enroll only one member of a given profession. Because members get to know each other very well, they are able to introduce their customers and other people to members of their networking group. For example, if they encounter someone who needs an accountant to do their taxes, a chapter member can say, *I meet weekly in a networking group with an accountant. She's a great person, and she provides excellent service. Can I give you her card?*

Eager to boost referrals to my Life & Career Coaching service, I joined this group. During my few years of membership, I tried two different chapters. In one chapter, I barely generated enough business to pay my membership cost, and the second group was almost a complete bust in terms of profit.

So when measured in terms of referrals and revenue generated, my membership in this networking group was a resounding failure. Yet, I'm very clear that my participation was an excellent experience that helped me greatly.

How can that be?

Well first, in weekly group meetings, there was always "networking education." This education provided excellent tips about networking in general, which I've used myself and taught to my clients. Second, I developed and practiced my first *elevator pitch*, which is a brief introduction to my services that can be delivered in the time it takes for a typical elevator ride (30 seconds). Third, during the course of my membership, I developed marketing language and techniques that greatly improved my ability to reach out to potential clients. Finally, I met some wonderful folks who are my friends to this day.

In summary, I didn't get direct referrals and revenue from the experience. Instead, I received information and skills that I've since used to generate more revenue on my own. Membership in the networking group gave my marketing a great tune up.

It just goes to show you that you never know how you're going to benefit from a particular experience. Sometimes you have to jump in and try it before you can discover opportunities.

Now, make that final plea to your Jury...
Feel this story's truth. Clear your mind, and breathe deeply. Now ask yourself: *What kind of person do I intend to be right now? What do I need to do to feel proud of myself when I'm done?*

Continue breathing deeply — Make a decision — Act!

*Back to **Enjoying the journey of life** (page 227)*

Winning the tournament

Defense Attorney's story for your Jury...

Back in the 90s, I joined a C-level recreational softball league. I'd never played any kind of baseball before, and it took a few seasons before I felt really comfortable with the sport.

One of the best parts of playing softball was participating in tournaments. My Boston-based teams traveled to places like Toronto, Montreal, Minneapolis, Washington DC, Chicago, New York, Atlanta, and San Diego to play softball and to have a good time.

Most of the tournaments held games on the Saturday and Sunday of a three-day weekend. We'd often play approximately three round-robin games, and then we'd enter a double-elimination tournament, which means that, if we lost two games, we were done. Some of the guys jokingly referred to this type of tournament as: *One, two, barbecue.*

During the first several years, I played for a team that wasn't very good. As a result, we never made it to the second day of play. I remember one year in Atlanta, they decided to start the Saturday games at noon instead of 8 or 9 am. That plan was undone by thunderstorms that rolled in during the early afternoon, creating a huge rain delay. I remember losing for the second time at 4 am and wondering how the heck the winning team was going to be able to get out of bed to play the first Sunday game, which was due to begin in only six hours!

I really wanted to experience being a tournament champion. I'd been to the banquets and seen the winning teams receiving their trophies. I wanted to know how it felt to bask in that kind of glory.

Well, I eventually switched teams, and my new team had considerably more talent. As luck would have it, I wouldn't have to wait long to find out what it was like to win a tournament; we won in Toronto during the first year with my new team.

The first hurdle was making it to the second day of play. The next hurdle was overcoming the fact that the first team we played on Sunday had scouted our hitting patterns, yet we knew nothing about where their players liked to hit the ball. To throw them off, we decided that we'd switch jerseys for the game, rendering all of their scouting data useless.

We were thrilled that our little scheme led to winning the first game on Sunday, and our spirits, energy, and enthusiasm remained high. We enjoyed every subsequent game, and winning that last game on Sunday was a thrill, but it wasn't at all what I expected.

Let me explain....

First, there were fewer teams at the field on Sunday than had been there on Saturday, of course. Then, as each team was knocked out of the tournament, they did what I used to do when I played for my previous team: we'd drive back to the hotel, shower, nap, and then hit the town for some fun. So as we won each game on Sunday, we played for a smaller and smaller audience.

Finally, this tournament made the unusual decision to hold the banquet on Saturday night, before all the games had been played. So after we won the championship game in front of a massive audience of eight people, the tournament director handed us our trophies on the field. No spotlight, no music, no applause, no glory.

Yay?!

After we returned home to Boston, we had a few weeks of bragging rights within our own league that we'd won the Toronto tournament, and then the thrill of victory faded away. It was onto more regular season games and another tournament later in the season.

*   *   *

Everyone has heard the expression, *It's the journey, not the destination.* The Toronto championship was one of my clearest lessons about this philosophy.

Out foxing that team first thing on Sunday morning was a thrill that I remember to this day. I have extremely fond memories of the friendships I formed with that group of guys, and I'm still friends with a few of them. It was tremendous fun getting to the second day of play, winning those Sunday games, and then handling the pressure of a championship game.

Yet, when it comes to the glory, the thrill of victory at the end, or the status of being "champions," the experience was kind of a bust. Good thing we had a blast getting to the end, because the end itself wasn't all that great.

I often say to my Life & Career Coaching clients that we spend days, weeks, months, and sometimes years working our way toward a goal, and we spend a tiny fraction of that time celebrating the victory. Given that we spend the vast majority of our time striving, it's best if we learn how to *enjoy every step* along the way.

Now, make that final plea to your Jury...

Feel this story's truth. Clear your mind, and breathe deeply. Now ask yourself: *What kind of person do I intend to be right now? What do I need to do to feel proud of myself when I'm done?*

Continue breathing deeply — Make a decision — Act!

*Back to **Enjoying the journey of life*** (page 227)

Focusing

Pivot away from anxiety and overwhelm, and into focusing on just the task at hand.

Pivot Inspirations:

- *It's like making love* (page 240)

- *"It's the economy, stupid"* (page 243)

- *Rock climber* (page 245)

- *Show yourself positive pictures* (page 249)

- *Visible, measurable goals* (page 252)

- *What can you do right now?* (page 256)

It's like making love

Defense Attorney's story for your Jury...
When my Life & Career Coaching clients are worried about performing well—for example, on a hot date, while interviewing for a great job, or while delivering an important presentation—I tell this story to help them understand *peak performance*. (Athletes call this "getting into the zone.")

In the movie *Bull Durham*, the baseball player Crash Davis is spending time at the batting cages as a way to work his way out of a slump. While practicing hitting, he's chatting with Anny Savoy. The chemistry and flirtatiousness between them is intense, but Annie is currently dating a young rookie on the team and has told Crash that she's not interested in him. (She says, *Despite my rejection of most Judeo-Christian ethics, I am, within the framework of the baseball season,* **monogamous**.)

As Crash tries to convince Annie to drop the rookie and go out with him, his batting gets worse as he becomes more agitated. Eventually, Annie attempts to point out the flaws in his stance. He mocks the idea that she has anything to teach him about hitting a baseball, yet she convinces him to give her the bat so she can demonstrate.

As she steps into the batter's box to show Crash a thing or two about hip placement, Annie says, *Making love is like hitting a baseball: you just gotta relax and concentrate.*

*   *   *

When helping my clients weave mindfulness approaches into their lives, I often remind them that they've already had this experience. During a very good love making session and a terrific day on vacation, everyone has felt that wonderful combination of relaxation, concentration, being in the moment, and just flowing sensually and smoothly with whatever is currently happening.

Also, as a former athlete, I know exactly what Annie is talking about. Some of my best athletic performances have occurred when I was able to get into the zone by relaxing and concentrating. When that happens, it's almost as if you don't have to think about anything. You click into a groove, and you just do what's needed right in that moment.

In Positive Psychology, there's a concept called *flow*. Flow experiences are times when you're working on a task that requires skill and goal setting, you're very connected and engaged with what you're doing (you *care*), and you lose yourself and all sense of time as you try to complete the task (*where did the time, go?*).[47] Flow is a specific kind of mindfulness, and it's the experience of "getting into the zone" for non-athletes.

Applying the yin-yang principle, you don't want to be too relaxed (you won't be sharp) or concentrate too intensely (you'll be stressed out); you want to blend the two together for optimal results.

When facing any task, practice relaxing and concentrating as you do it. Then when you're facing an important, high-stakes task, you'll be well practiced and better able to slip into that peak-performance groove. *It's just like making love.*

Now, make that final plea to your Jury...

Feel this story's truth. Clear your mind, and breathe deeply. Now ask yourself: *What kind of person do I intend to be right now? What do I need to do to feel proud of myself when I'm done?*

Continue breathing deeply — Make a decision — Act!

Back to **Focusing** (page 239)

"It's the economy, stupid"

Defense Attorney's story for your Jury...
In 1992, Bill Clinton was running for president against George H. W. Bush. At that time, it was very challenging for a Democratic candidate to win the presidency of the United States. The Republicans had held the office for twelve years, with Ronald Reagan having been a very popular president. Also during the first Iraq War, President H. W. Bush's approval rating was sky high.

When running for president, a candidate needs to address an incredibly wide variety of issues and appeal to a huge number of people. That person is expected to eat everything from corn dogs in Iowa to crawfish in Louisiana, understand the intricacies of foreign policy across the entire world, remark on pop culture, understand all sorts of arcane financial situations and their effect on the economy, take natural and appealing selfies with voters, and recite all sorts of statistics at a moment's notice. It's a potentially *overwhelming* challenge!

Well during the campaign, Clinton strategist James Carville understood that not all issues were equally important in terms of winning the election, and he needed to find a way to help both his candidate and campaign workers to maintain a tight focus on what was most important. So during a strategy meeting, he hung a sign in campaign headquarters that listed the three more important focal points, with "The economy, stupid" being the most memorable.[48]

Bill Clinton won that election in 1992, and addressing economic concerns was a major factor in achieving victory.

This tactic was so noteworthy and successful that the phrase is still used today to mean, *Let's not be foolish and lose focus. Let's get back to what's most important.*

*   *   *

A few things stand out in this story. First, when it comes to your Defense Attorney using striking, compelling language to sway your Jury, notice the difference between saying *Let's not be foolish and lose focus* and *It's the economy, stupid!* There's no contest in terms of impact.

Another key to success is that this message was delivered in the form of a visual reminder: a sign that people saw every day as they entered their workplace. You can use post-its, index cards, phone apps, and more to keep an important message "in your face."

Finally, this is a great example of reducing potentially long and complex conversations to one catchy phrase. My Zen Driving story described how I reduced years of thought and effort to *no harm, no foul.* The civil rights movement in the United States during the 50s and 60s used a similarly catchy phrase that underlines the importance of staying focused: *keep your eyes on the prize.*

Now, make that final plea to your Jury...

Feel this story's truth. Clear your mind, and breathe deeply. Now ask yourself: *What kind of person do I intend to be right now? What do I need to do to feel proud of myself when I'm done?*

Continue breathing deeply — Make a decision — Act!

*Back to **Focusing** (page 239)*

Rock climber

Defense Attorney's story for your Jury…

Picture this TV scene: a close-up shot of a lean, athletic-looking woman in the middle of a rock climbing adventure. You can see her feet firmly planted, and one of her hands looks securely clasped onto a slight ledge.

The question right now is obvious. *Where is she going to grasp with her one free hand?* Her face is the picture of concentration, scanning the surface, trying to find something to grip. She's level headed and systematic. Perhaps she's moving her hand along the surface of the stone, trying to feel for something to leverage. Maybe she's cocking her head back slightly so as to visually scan for opportunities.

It's at this point when the camera pulls back, and we see that *she's hanging off the side of a cliff!* The wider camera angle reveals blue sky, other mountain tops, and more mountain surface to climb. Just to freak out the viewers at home, the camera might pan down, showing how far she could possibly fall. *Yikes!*

Sitting on my couch witnessing this scene on the TV, I'm a mixture of dumbfounded, exhilarated, and terrified. I can't imagine ever doing something like that. *How the heck does she do it? What if she falls? How frustrating is it that she's nowhere near the top yet?*

Then, the camera zooms back in for another close-up, and the sky, the potential fall, and the rest of the mountain disappear from view. The climber has secured her free hand, and now it's time for her to find a new, slightly higher location for one of her feet. Just as we saw before, she evaluates and tests her options, remaining completely focused just on the rock, cracks, ledges, and surfaces available within a foot or two. Her body and the rocky surface within reach are all that exist *in her world* right now.

Keenly observing her up close and personal, the secret occurs to me. *No one climbs a mountain.* Just as this woman does, they find a way to move a single hand or foot. Then, they do it again. And again. *And again.* As a result of all these small actions, the mountain eventually gets climbed.

Now, I have no expertise with rock climbing. Notwithstanding, those of us watching at home can observe some of her decision-making process. Maybe there's no ledge or crack, and she has to hammer a spike into the rock, so she can then grip it or run her rope through it. Maybe a quick visual scan reveals she has to alter her course to the right or left to find a more hospitable climbing surface. Perhaps she needs to move down before she can adjust left or right before climbing back up. It might be time to secure her tent into the side of the mountain with spikes so she can get some sleep before the next day's climb.

Can I grip a ledge with my hand? **Yes.** *Can I hammer one spike?* **Yes.** *Can I locate a position for my left foot?* **Yes.** *Can I take the first step in adjusting my course to the left?* **Yep!**

One decision at a time, she focuses on it and gets it done. All the while giving no attention to how far she might fall, how much further she has to climb, or the beauty of the blue sky and the birds flying at her level. There will be time for that after she's completed the climb. No need to distract or paralyze herself with the big picture right at this moment.

She moves another foot, makes another decision, hammers a spike, slips her fingers into a crack, and on and on, until she's at the top of the mountain, raising her fists triumphantly into the thin air.

*   *   *

Of course, most of us don't tackle extreme projects such as mountain climbing. I sure as heck don't. Yet, what are the "mountains" in our lives that are intimidating us? In our more ordinary lives, when are we scaring ourselves with how far we might fall, depressing ourselves with how far we have to go, or anxiously distracting ourselves due to avoidance?

In moments like this, inspire yourself with the story of the mountain climber. Rededicate yourself to moving just one foot, adjusting one hand, or making a decision to alter your path. Give that one small action your *full attention*, and *DO* it!

If she can do it with a *mountain*, you can do it with dating, changing your career, losing weight, or any other personal project that needs doing.

Now, make that final plea to your Jury...

Feel this story's truth. Clear your mind, and breathe deeply. Now ask yourself: *What kind of person do I intend to be right now? What do I need to do to feel proud of myself when I'm done?*

Continue breathing deeply — Make a decision — Act!

Back to **Focusing** (page 239)

Show yourself positive pictures

Defense Attorney's story for your Jury...
Imagine that I was able to follow you all day, every day, and I managed to show you pictures—providing descriptive narrations, playing creepy background music, showing video—of everything that's horrifying and negative about life. For example, I'd make you watch scenes of famine, poverty, war, painful death, torture, genocide, disease, abuse, rape, cruelty, and natural disasters. Again, you wouldn't be able to get away from it. It would be "in your face" during every waking moment.

Clearly, you'd break down under the horrific emotional weight. I certainly would. (For a cinematic take on what this exercise might be like, see the rehabilitation scenes at the end of the movie *A Clockwork Orange*.)

Now, let's change it up. Imagine instead that I was able to follow you around all day, every day, showing you pictures of the very best of humanity and life: love, compassion, advances in science, people providing a helping hand, love, cooperation, togetherness, doctors curing diseases, generosity, families reuniting, and natural beauty.

Of course, being bombarded by positive images would put a pep in your step.

Just so that we're clear, this is not an exercise about being correct or incorrect, about anything being true or false. The negative images are just as "correct" and "true" as the positive

249

ones. It's not as if I'm lying about anything when I show the horrible pictures.

More to the point is the emotional effect of maintaining one focus versus another. If you can maintain a positive focus—a realistic one that emphasizes hope, flexibility, and manageability, and that avoids a Pollyanna approach—then that should leave you with enough energy to reach goals, solve problems, improve less-than-optimal situations, and build the life you've dreamed of having.

Don't focus in a way that debilitates and shuts you down; focus in a way that energizes and supports your success.

*   *   *

What are areas in your life or situations you face in which you often lock onto an unhelpful, limiting, or draining focus? What are situations in your life that result in you locking onto an unhelpful focus? To get out of this jam, practice taking a negative observation, and flipping it to a realistic and positive one. For example, you can focus on:

- The difficult situation being temporary.

- Actions you can take to make the situation better.

- Just focus on today's tasks, making an overwhelming long-term situation feel more manageable.

- Whom you might ask for help.

- How your situation is much better than those faced by others or better than your own situation in the past.

- Times when you've gotten yourself out of similar jams.

- Your ability to learn and develop skills needed to fix the situation.

- Phrasing words so that you stay as positive as possible while still being truthful about the challenges you face.

- How the difficult situation is not the sum total of every part of life, that you can still feel the sunshine, walk around in a healthy body, enjoy a laugh, succeed at other tasks, maintain wonderful relationships, or rest in the comforting arms of a loved one.

- The fact that others of similar intelligence and resources have gotten out of this jam, so you can as well.

By focusing on solutions, methods of coping, respite breaks, assistance, hope, and manageability, it's the equivalent of you walking around showing yourself positive pictures all day, and you'll feel the increase in your ability to take action and move forward.

Now, make that final plea to your Jury...
Feel this story's truth. Clear your mind, and breathe deeply. Now ask yourself: *What kind of person do I intend to be right now? What do I need to do to feel proud of myself when I'm done?*

Continue breathing deeply — Make a decision — Act!

Back to **Focusing** (page 239)

Visible, measurable goals

While working on this book, I set a goal to write every Sunday for at least three hours. For the most part, I completed chapters in Part I in good time. Clearly, I was following the suggestion that proper goals need to be both *observable* and *measurable*; someone could see whether I was at my laptop every Sunday and if I remained there for at least three hours.

Check! Goal met.

However, after a few months of working on the short Pivot Inspiration stories, progress felt slower. On average, I was finishing only two or three stories a week. As a result, I realized that maintaining my current pace would mean that I wouldn't finish the Pivot Inspirations for another two and a half months.

Two and a half months? ***That's too slow!***

So, I decided to make a few adjustments. First, I set *daily writing goals* and placed them in my electronic calendar, which I can see on both my tablet and smart phone. I put an "appointment" into the calendar for every evening at 8 p.m. stating the number of Pivot Inspirations I planned on writing that day. Then, at the end of the day, I'd edit the appointment and note how many I actually wrote. So, a notation of "4/3" meant that I'd planned on writing four, and I actually wrote three.

In this way, every time I looked at my calendar, I would see a visual reminder—a *cue*—that I needed to be writing that day and how much I expected to produce. My success or failure in reaching those numbers was unavoidably "in my face."

Second, I decided to place my gym routine on hold for a few weeks while I made writing a higher priority. This was a temporary, minor setback for my exercise goal, but it freed approximately 10 hours of time each week for writing.

Finally, I decided to set higher goals than I had accomplished previously. I did some soul searching, and I asked myself how many stories I could write if I stopped lollygagging by obsessively re-wording and editing the text. I ultimately decided that, if I had a full afternoon available to write, I should be able to complete six Pivot Inspirations, double my previous maximum output.

Well, the resulting boost in productivity was *amazing*. In the first week using my new calendar-reminder method, I completed 22 stories. After returning to the gym the following week, I was on pace to complete between five and ten stories weekly; even with my gym routine back in place, I was doubling and sometimes tripling my output using new methods that helped me to focus better.

*   *   *

The next time you feel disappointed with your output and it feels as if you're procrastinating, dragging your feet, or getting distracted, consider that the *distractions* might not be the problem. Maybe it's the *cues* that are too weak or improperly placed. If you have better ways of focusing, then the distractions might not feel so compelling.

Given the previous calendar-reminder story, here are some ways to evaluate and tune-up your process:

- Make sure that reminders are located in the right place, so you'll see them right when you need them.

- Make sure that you're observing and measuring in ways that boost productivity.

- I was focused on the day and number of hours, when instead I needed to be focused on writing a *certain number of stories weekly*.

- Test your limits; don't settle for what's comfortable. Expect more from yourself, and then make the effort to match that expectation.

  When I faced my first six-story day, I felt somewhat intimidated, yet also excited to give it a try. I surprised myself and was able to complete all six. I found that I wrote faster, and I allowed myself only one or two editing passes instead of obsessing for 45 minutes over minor word choices. The next time I faced a goal of six stories, I challenged myself to set a new personal best, and I was able to complete *seven!* For the next few days after that, it was very motivating to see that 6/7 notation.

- Make sure that your system boosts motivation instead of lowering it.

For example, I needed to remind myself that, even though a 6/3 output was technically a "failure" in that I didn't reach my daily goal, it was a "wild success" in terms of me being able to write ten or more stories every week.

Now, make that final plea to your Jury...
Feel this story's truth. Clear your mind, and breathe deeply. Now ask yourself: *What kind of person do I intend to be right now? What do I need to do to feel proud of myself when I'm done?*

Continue breathing deeply — Make a decision — Act!

Back to **Focusing** (page 239)

What can you do right now?

Defense Attorney's story for your Jury...
In 2007, I had very successful surgery on a herniated disc. It was the end of a near year-long ordeal of pain, progressive decline in my physical ability, frustration dealing with the medical system, and...did I mention the pain?

There were several times during that year when I missed work, the longest being the last month and a half before surgery. During that time, my days consisted of getting out of bed, using a cane to get to the living room, lying down on the floor, remaining there until nighttime, and then using my cane to go to bed.

When I'd get sore or numb lying on the floor, I'd shift 180 degrees and lie in the opposite direction, which gave me relief and some comfort. When I needed to go to the bathroom, I'd use my cane. I bathed only twice during that time, kneeling with one hand in the tub, both of my knees outside of it, using my free hand to apply a wash cloth. Showering was just too painful.

Every morning after I positioned myself on the floor, my husband would toss me a bagged lunch before leaving for work. At night, I'd prop myself up, balancing on my calloused elbows in a director's chair, and I'd have dinner with him, returning to the floor immediately after I'd finished my food.

I watched a lot of daytime TV. *George, you are NOT the father of Jessica's baby! [hysterics ensue]* I read a little bit, but the pain medication restricted my ability to concentrate, especially in the first hour after taking it. I had my music. I could meditate. I ran through my collection of DVDs, which included a few multi-disc sets.

Today, if someone made me lie on the floor all day in front of the TV, I'd be concerned about going stir crazy. Yet, when I reflect on the six weeks before my surgery, I was a reasonably happy guy. Seriously!

In my opinion, the secret to me maintaining a good mood was focusing tightly on *what I was able to do*, resisting the temptation to focus on things *I'd **rather** be doing*, and making the absolute most out of my available options. So for example, watching TV, reading, meditating, and seeing movies aren't bad activities, right? There's nothing difficult or stressful about them. There's fun there. Not *wild* fun, but fun nonetheless.

Now, I'm human, and my mind wandered occasionally. I might think, *What if I never get better and live the rest of my life crippled?* or *What if I die or become paralyzed on the operating table?* or *I really wish I could get back to my technical writing job so I can help with an important project*. It was clear to me when I lost focus, because I'd feel bad. When that happened, I'd scamper back to my emotional "safe place" of eating, bathroom breaks, TV, movies, books, and meditating.

When comparing the two different ways of focusing, it was crystal clear to me which one made me feel better. It was a deal I made with myself back then: *I'm going to focus on, think about, and do **only these** things, OK?!*

Immediately after surgery, my husband was amazed at how I climbed down from the gurney, reclined slowly in a chair, and had dinner with him sitting up without pain for the first time in months. Only then did I allow my focus to return to bigger and better things.

*   *   *

Obviously, being almost completely immobile for six weeks is an extreme situation. That being said, how many times do we suffer and make ourselves miserable by focusing on *what we wish we could do* instead of *what we are **able** to do*? Or, how many times do we focus on how things might go wrong in the future instead of paying close attention to doing everything in this moment to make things go right?

In a way, my extreme experience was a lesson in accepting what I was able to do and letting go of everything else. Day to day, my "job," if you will, was to pay attention to my body, keep it comfortable, and occupy my mind as best I can.

If it was something I could do, then I gave it my attention, engagement, and complete acceptance. If it was something I had no control over, then it was "beyond my pay grade," and I gave it almost no mind, shifting my focus.

At any time, you can go to your ever-present safe place: relax, accept, and engage only with what's right in front of you. When you're able to do more, you will. Until then, remove those other options from your awareness.

Now, make that final plea to your Jury...

Feel this story's truth. Clear your mind, and breathe deeply. Now ask yourself: *What kind of person do I intend to be right now? What do I need to do to feel proud of myself when I'm done?*

Continue breathing deeply — Make a decision — Act!

Back to **Focusing** (page 239)

Letting go of control

Pivot away from anxious need to over-control, and into relaxation and acceptance.

Pivot Inspirations:

- *Give up control to get control* (page 262)

- *Let the ball tell you where to hit it* (page 265)

- *Ordering Chinese food at a pizza place* (page 269)

- *Surf it* (page 272)

Give up control to get control

Defense Attorney's story for your Jury...

As a child tennis player in the 1970s, I was a huge fan of Chris Evert, and I loved to root for her against Martina Navratilova. In recent years, I discovered a wonderful book that described their battles, *The Rivals: Chris Evert vs. Martina Navratilova Their Epic Duels and Extraordinary Friendship*, by Johnette Howard.

Now, there was one situation depicted in the book that I want to highlight, though let me first convey a young fan's impression of Evert in the mid-to-late 1970s. I'll begin by saying that her nickname was *Chris America*. Blond, smart, pretty, polite, talented, and ladylike, she was embraced far and wide.

On the court, beginning at a very young age, she won...and won and won some more. Her style was one of precision and control, painting the lines with her shots. "Machine like" would be a fair description of her play. She wore a stoic, expressionless look on her face—though you could tell she was upset when she pursed her lips and her neck muscles tightened. She always remained gracious, always following protocol.

Chris dated famous men, movie stars and top tennis players. She was a natural for endorsements. I particularly remember her sipping ice tea on a TV commercial. She was famous, rich, and traveled the world.

...and she was also frequently miserable.

The anecdote in the book that stood out for me was one in which Chris, during a tournament, was walking down the darkened entrance tunnel to the stadium, and she just had to stop, slump into a seated position against a wall, and break down into a good crying jag before entering the court to play.

In very brief summary, if I had to point to one thing underlying the breakdown, it would be Chris focusing almost exclusively on not losing (she *hated* losing), which meant that she derived no pleasure from winning. After victories, the best she felt was relieved.

After years of being able to will and control her way to extraordinary success, she couldn't do it any longer. As I say to my Life & Career Coaching clients, you might be able to get better performance by whipping the horse with one stroke, but if you do it too much then the horse will eventually buck and refuse to run.

Toward the end of the decade and in response to Martina roaring past her in ability, Chris decided to...well...lighten up. She allowed people to see her emotions more often, appearing more playful and even goofy. She sacrificed some of her "girl next door" looks to hit the gym, build muscle, and become more athletic in order to compete better with Martina. She even took more risks with her style of play, leaving the safety of the baseline to make riskier plays at the net.

As a result, she seemed to blossom emotionally; she just *looked happier*. Also, her game improved as well, leading to some extraordinary matches with Martina in the early-to-mid 80s.

The irony was unmistakable. In order to get *better*, Chris had to stop trying to be *perfect*. She had to *let go of control* in order to *regain control*.

Now, make that final plea to your Jury...
Feel this story's truth. Clear your mind, and breathe deeply. Now ask yourself: *What kind of person do I intend to be right now? What do I need to do to feel proud of myself when I'm done?*

Continue breathing deeply — Make a decision — Act!

Back to **Letting go of control** (page 261)

Let the ball tell you where to hit it

Defense Attorney's story for your Jury…

Although I was an all-around jock in my youth, I'd never played organized baseball until I was thirty years old. In an effort to boost my social life at that time, I joined a C-level recreational softball team. The idea was to meet people and to have a good time, but it wasn't long before my competitive nature took over.

Now, at 6' 5", I'm best suited for the outfield or first base. That being said, the coaches were having a difficult time finding someone athletic enough to play short stop, one of the most difficult positions on the field. So, they had me try out for that position, and it led to a decade of me being a utility infielder. I even earned the nickname *Tallstop*.

Those familiar with baseball understand that a shortstop is primarily valued for his defense, so it's often the case that that player bats near the bottom of the order and is not expected to contribute much scoring. The shortstop's main value is in the field, not at the plate.

During a decade-long stint, my batting patterns changed. Initially, I hit everything hard and far to left field, which is common for a novice player who is right handed. I then learned how to hit the ball to the opposite field. Finally, I began hitting the ball up the middle.

Unfortunately, my batting average deteriorated year to year. At first, I was putting pressure on myself to hit the ball into new parts of the field. Then, I was putting pressure on myself to hit the ball wherever I saw a gap in the field. As my batting percentage got lower and lower, I then began to pressure myself into *just getting a hit.* By my seventh year in the league, I was the worst hitter on my team and batting .180 (less than two hits for every 10 times at bat), which is *horrible* for slow pitch, ten-foot-arch softball.

My teammates and coaches were great and very supportive. Yet, I couldn't shake the feeling that I was a burden to them. I didn't have to be a *great* hitter, but I really wanted not to stink so badly.

 I remember when I finally made my breakthrough. Frustrated with the stress of trying so hard, I approached the plate this one time, and I just didn't have it in me to get all intense again. I remember letting go, taking deep and relaxing breaths, and suddenly not caring. Standing peacefully in the batter's box at the plate, it was in this very quiet mental place that a thought occurred to me: *let the ball tell you where to hit it.*

Hmmm!

I was off the hook. I didn't need to worry or press. I didn't need to "figure it out." I didn't need to try anything fancy. All I needed to do was obey the trajectory of the ball.

From that point forward, I looked at every pitch, and I asked myself where that particular ball could best be hit. If it was too high, too close, or too far away from me, I'd let it go. (Sometimes one of those pitches would be called for a strike, but I didn't care. That ball told me *not* to hit it.) If the ball was close to me, it was telling me to pull it to left field. If it required a bit of a stretch, it was hinting that I needed to go opposite, to right field. Balls that were coming down around my shoulders convinced me to hit line drives; lower balls shouted to be turned into ground balls.

I remember that, once I got used to this new way of batting, it seemed as if the pitched softball sat in the air *forever*, giving me more than enough time to figure out what to do with it.

At the end of my final season, I was batting .670 (almost seven hits for every 10 times at bat), and I was the second-best batter on the team. One or two more hits that season, and I would have been *the best*. I'm just sayin'...!

*   *   *

I often tell my Life & Career Coaching clients that sometimes it's a matter of getting out of our own way. We may have notions about what we want to do, but it may not be what's called for in that particular situation. If we can put aside our egos—our wants, desires, fears, and needs—and if we can relax and concentrate on what is unfolding right in front of us, then the situation will reveal possibilities; it will point to the necessary next step.

Put down your ideas of where you "should" hit the ball; instead, let it tell you where to hit it.

Now, make that final plea to your Jury...
Feel this story's truth. Clear your mind, and breathe deeply. Now ask yourself: *What kind of person do I intend to be right now? What do I need to do to feel proud of myself when I'm done?*

Continue breathing deeply — Make a decision — Act!

Back to **Letting go of control** (page 261)

Ordering Chinese food at a pizza place

Defense Attorney's story for your Jury...
The yin-and-yang of control is to apply it when you have it and let it go when you don't. If you find yourself having trouble accepting a situation and "going with it," you can think of this story about ordering Chinese food in a pizza shop.

Imagine walking into a pizza parlor, and the woman behind the counter smiles and waits patiently for you to scan the menu for something that looks appetizing. Feeling disappointed, you ask yourself what you're in the mood for, and you decide that Chinese food would be really delicious right about now. So, you ask the women behind the counter if she has any pork fried rice, pot stickers, General Tso's Chicken, or Lo Mein.

Let's assume that you've encountered *the nicest*, most *patient* pizza-shop server on the planet. She considers your question for a second or two, smiles, and then says, *Unfortunately, no, but we do have pizza and Italian dishes here*!

You sigh heavily and try to explain how much you'd really love to have some Chinese food right now. Couldn't she just make an exception and whip up some?

At this point, the proprietor is looking amused. She says, *Well, we do serve spaghetti. That's **really close** to Lo Mein. Could I interest you in some nice spaghetti and meatballs, maybe with a side of garlic bread?*

269

You scrunch your nose and explain how that's *just not the same.* You continue to plead your case. *Couldn't you please, please,* **pretty please** *cook the spaghetti in a Lo mein recipe?* You seem oblivious to the growing irritation of the customers in line behind you.

At this point, even though the pizza-shop woman is super nice, she's beginning to understand that she won't be able to please you. She explains how she doesn't have the expertise, spices, and sauces used to make a really nice Chinese dish. She then points out that the Panda Wok down the street makes some really nice Lo Mein. Perhaps you can give them some business tonight and then come back when you're in the mood for some great pizza, calzones, or pasta.

Again, you make a face, exhale loudly, and tell her that it's a really cold winter night out there, and it really would work much better for you if she could just whip up some Chinese food right here.

The woman behind the counter then plants an emotionless smile on her face, says that she's sorry that she can't help you tonight, and asks you to step aside, please, so she can help the next customer in line.

You're dissatisfied. The proprietor is dissatisfied. The people in line behind you are grumpy and dissatisfied. Nobody wins.

*   *   *

Of course, this is an absurd example. Yet how many times have we spent a huge amount of time and energy trying to bend a situation to our will when it wasn't possible or when others around us weren't willing to go along?

Continuing with our restaurant example, it's perfectly fine for you to ask for what you want, even if it's "not on the menu." For example, I read recently that a restaurant had a member of its staff run to the market across the street to buy fresh eggplant so they could satisfy a customer request. Or I've heard of restaurants making a PB&J sandwich or scrambling eggs for someone, even though those items weren't on the menu; they had the ingredients, and they did their best to please.

During those times when a situation can't or won't accommodate you, either gracefully and politely make your exit, or surrender, accept, and make the most out of what's being offered. Remember that putting your needs aside, going along with the situation as it is, and *making the most of it* can strengthen relationships (you're being a good team player in this instance), or it can expose you to something unexpectedly wonderful and new. Periodically, let go, get into it, and give it your all, even if it's not what you originally intended.

Now, make that final plea to your Jury...
Feel this story's truth. Clear your mind, and breathe deeply. Now ask yourself: *What kind of person do I intend to be right now? What do I need to do to feel proud of myself when I'm done?*
Continue breathing deeply — Make a decision — Act!

*Back to **Letting go of control** (page 261)*

Surf it

In many respects, control is an illusion. We think we have it, we're sure we can get it, we're unnerved when we're out of it. That's a lot of angst and upset over something that often doesn't exist.

To put your desire for control into perspective, put aside your desire for complete control, and instead do your best *to surf* the situation.

For example, once you're out in the water and waiting for a good wave, there's a lot that's not within your control. You can't control the ocean or its waves.

Before entering the water that day, you could have controlled your choice of surf board or how long you practiced to build skill. But time for that has long past; you're left with the board you've chosen and your current skill level. It'll do you no good to wish you could change these things right at this moment.

Just to give you a few more examples, you don't control the water temperature, the weather, the wind, or the presence of other surfers. You are not privy to information about how and when that wave will break.

So, you've got *no* control, right? You're "out of control"?

Nope.

You get to choose which wave you'll attempt to ride. You time your jump onto the board. You determine how to move your arms and shift your weight so as to maintain your balance. You need to keep an eye on the wave, determining when to cut underneath it as it breaks. There are dozens and dozens of decisions and adjustments that are needed for a fun, successful surfing of a wave.

So, be a good sport about everything that you can't control, relax, and surf the situation. Make wise choices, adjust here, adjust there, lean forward, lean back, and ride that wave to completion.

Now, make that final plea to your Jury...
Feel this story's truth. Clear your mind, and breathe deeply. Now ask yourself: *What kind of person do I intend to be right now? What do I need to do to feel proud of myself when I'm done?*

Continue breathing deeply — Make a decision — Act!

Back to **Letting go of control** (page 261)

Making decisions

Pivot away from struggling with decisions, and into a relaxed approach.

Pivot Inspirations:

- *"Don't jump yet...waaait for it..."* (page 276)

- *Make room on the table* (page 278)

- *Put it on the back burner* (page 281)

- *Two team members need to get on the same page* (page 284)

- *Wait until the answer finds you* (page 286)

"Don't jump yet... *waaait for it...*"

Defense Attorney's story for your Jury...
When it comes to making a decision, I often think of those old movies, the ones with stowaways on a train who have to jump before it arrives at the next station.

In some movies, they jump, land on some grass, and roll down an embankment (someone *always* sprains an ankle). I've seen at least one movie in which they leap off a train bridge and into water below: don't try that one at home, folks!

On the one hand, you can't jump too soon, because you don't want to face plant into a tree, splatter yourself against a wall, or land on some sharp rocks. You need to find that grassy embankment or water landing. So, it's important to pay close attention, evaluating the terrain ahead of you.

On the other hand, you don't have all day. If you don't take advantage of an opportunity before the train reaches the next station, you'll be apprehended.

In those movies, I often think of two young people, clutching hands, intensely focusing on the land alongside the tracks. They're at the edge of the open door to the boxcar, ready to jump.

They're both keenly alert, and they know they need to time the jump just right.

You can hear one murmur, *Waaait for it...wait for it....*

*   *   *

When you're facing a decision that must be made soon, simultaneously maintain concentration and think to yourself, *Waaait for it...waaait for it...*as a way to maintain your readiness without jumping too soon.

*   *   *

Now, make that final plea to your Jury...

Feel this story's truth. Clear your mind, and breathe deeply. Now ask yourself: *What kind of person do I intend to be right now? What do I need to do to feel proud of myself when I'm done?*

Continue breathing deeply — Make a decision — Act!

Back to **Making decisions** (page 275)

Make room on the table

When my Life & Career Coaching clients talk about making a big decision, they often describe it as *hard work*—especially when it involves mulling it over, repeatedly analyzing it in their minds. People mistakenly think this is the way to get a great result. Instead, try thinking about a big decision as something that a person (your *subconscious mind*) brings to you and places onto your "table" (which is your *conscious mind*).

When people describe what it's like finally to make an important decision about something complex, they don't usually describe it as the direct result of thinking things through. Instead, they use language such as *it suddenly occurred to me,* or *a light bulb went off,* or *I don't know how, but I just knew.* During a clear moment, the decision pops into their awareness.

So, do your homework, create your lists of Pros (advantages) and Cons (disadvantages), talk it over with trusted loved ones, and do your Internet research. Be clear about what makes sense to you both logically and emotionally. Think of those activities as filling the table of your conscious mind with data and information that needs further attention.

Then, sleep on it a while and trust that your subconscious mind will remove all the research from your table and will bring it into its private office for further processing. Occupy yourself with other concerns and activities. Trust that your subconscious mind will get back to you when it's completed

278

its work. *Keep your conscious mind clear*, so you'll have a clear table top.

Two things happen when you relax and stop pushing toward a solution. First, in this more observant, peaceful state, you may notice new information that can lead to a better decision. (*I was listening to what you were saying, and it suddenly occurred to me what I needed to do.*) Second, because you've cleared your table of logic and worry and details, there's now room on your table top for a decision (*it just occurred to me out of nowhere!*).

Instead of forcing a new item onto a crowded table top, clear the clutter, first.

* * *

You may be reading this while thinking, *Easier said than done!* Well first of all, I didn't *say* it would be easy. The worry that drives you to hurry up and make a decision is the same thing that clutters your mental table, leaving little room for the decision to appear. It can be a Catch-22.

A great first step is literally to *sleep on it*, which means putting analysis aside for a while before making a decision. So, slowing down and inserting extra time into the process are short-term tactics that can yield some immediate results.

Second, establishing a mindfulness practice eventually increases your ability to stop pushing toward a solution and to be open to one that presents itself. This practice increases your ability to relax, to focus on the present moment (as opposed to worrying about when you'll come to a decision), and to participate in an activity while simultaneously staying in touch with how you're feeling about it.

Now, make that final plea to your Jury...
Feel this story's truth. Clear your mind, and breathe deeply. Now ask yourself: *What kind of person do I intend to be right now? What do I need to do to feel proud of myself when I'm done?*

Continue breathing deeply — Make a decision — Act!

Back to **Making decisions** (page 275)

Put it on the back burner

Defense Attorney's story for your Jury...
Years ago, I was vacationing in Williamsburg, Virginia. After having my first taste of Brunswick stew at a local restaurant, I perused the cookbooks on display near the exit. I wanted an authentic recipe so I could make a stew as good as the one I'd just tasted in the restaurant.

Mistrusting the glossy "corporate" cookbooks on display, I asked the clerk if there were any more, and she pointed me toward a small room behind the front desk. It was there that I found a Wire-O bound cookbook prepared by the Junior League of Jackson, Mississippi.

Score!

Their recipe originated before the Revolutionary War and was passed down through the generations. It called for the ingredients to be placed in a large cauldron and stirred using a boat oar. (I kid you not.) I had to buy a very large pot and then reduce the recipe to 1/16th the original size so it would all fit.

In the British tradition, Brunswick stew is one of those "toss it all in a pot and cook the heck out of it" types of dishes. It contains beef, pork, ham, chicken, and bacon. (*Bacon!!!*) It also contains stewed tomatoes, potatoes, carrots, and other veggies, including okra.

Success depends on adding ingredients gradually, hour after hour. The total cooking time is approximately six hours. I remember the first few times I made the stew, I struggled to keep the flame extremely low and to keep stirring the pot, so that food didn't burn and stick to the bottom.

It's delicious, but don't tell your doctor. It's not exactly *health* food.

*　　*　　*

You can cook some food fast, prepare some food in a moderate amount of time, and take hours or even days to make other types of dishes. No judgment; You just want to make sure that you're giving the dish the amount of time it needs.

I assist my Life & Career Coaching clients with some significant life changes and personal projects. Examples include deciding to get married, deciding to quit a job without a new one lined up, moving across the country, or deciding to divorce.

When it comes to complex decision-making, my clients sometimes wish they could wrap it up quickly (fry a hamburger), when what they really need is to sleep on it and let it unfold over time (make Brunswick stew).

I say to clients in these situations that they should put the decision on the back burner of their minds and turn the heat *way down low.* Next, do some research and preparation. Chop
up some meat, throw it into the pot, and let it stew. Later, chop up some potatoes, throw them into the pot, and let it stew some more.

Don't push. Don't try to "figure it out." Don't put any expectations on when the decision needs to be made.

Instead, let it simmer. Let it stew. Taste it from time to time to see how it's doing. *Let the food* tell you when it's ready.

Now, make that final plea to your Jury...

Feel this story's truth. Clear your mind, and breathe deeply. Now ask yourself: *What kind of person do I intend to be right now? What do I need to do to feel proud of myself when I'm done?*

Continue breathing deeply — Make a decision — Act!

Back to **Making decisions** (page 275)

Two team members need to get on the same page

When someone feels torn about a decision, it can be said that she's *ambivalent*, that she's *of two minds*. The yin-yang symbols used in *Daily Pivots* provide a handy illustration for a certain type of ambivalence (*on the **one** hand...but then again on the **other** hand*).

Sometimes, it's clear that you're of two minds; you're quite aware of the two options and both seem appealing in their own way. Sometimes, one desire is subconscious; you think that you know exactly what you want to do, but there's a deeper part of you who just seems to sabotage your efforts, perhaps with procrastination or distractions, or maybe by "freezing up" in fear when it's time to act.

When I'm working with a Life & Career Coaching client facing such a situation, I suggest that they look at it as if they have two teammates inside of them who are not in agreement, or "not on the same page" as they say. You can't make progress until everyone on "your team" is in agreement and working together.

So, treat this situation in the same way you would any interpersonal conflict interfering with efficient teamwork. Talk it out and negotiate an agreement.

The first step when attempting to negotiate well is to listen thoroughly to the "other side," and demonstrate that you understand and respect her concerns. For example, if you're procrastinating, imagine that one member of the team is balking because she has a valid but unspoken objection to doing the work right away. Hearing and respecting objections builds trust. Only after you have trust can you begin to discuss possible changes and make requests. For example, perhaps you can cut a deal that involves meeting her needs now, and she can meet your needs very soon afterward (*you scratch my back, and I'll scratch yours*).

When you're feeling stuck in ambivalence, it usually means that at least one part of you is refusing to cooperate until she feels heard. Show a little respect, apply it to your negotiations, and watch how quickly you can arrive at a win-win decision and get moving again.

Now, make that final plea to your Jury...
Feel this story's truth. Clear your mind, and breathe deeply. Now ask yourself: *What kind of person do I intend to be right now? What do I need to do to feel proud of myself when I'm done?*

Continue breathing deeply — Make a decision — Act!

Back to **Making decisions** (page 275)

Wait until the answer finds you

When my Life & Career Coaching clients talk about making a big decision, they often describe it as something that they have to search for and discover. Instead, flip it around. Think of a complex decision as something that needs to *find its way to you.*

So, do your homework, create your lists of Pros (advantages) and Cons (disadvantages), talk it over with trusted loved ones, and do your Internet research. Be clear about what makes sense to you both logically and emotionally. Think of those activities as drawing maps to your house.

For example, to make sure people can find my coaching practice, I create a website, put maps and directions on it, produce marketing materials, distribute my business card, get listed on the Directory in the lobby downstairs, and have a plaque next to my door that identifies my office. Now, I don't run out, find my clients, and escort them to my office; my clients use all of my preliminary work to find their way to me.

Big decisions about complex matters are similar. Once you broadcast the desired results, the decision will find you and present itself. Sometimes it makes itself known while you're doing something else that just happens to shed light (*I was listening to what you were saying, and it suddenly occurred to me what I needed to do!*). Sometimes, when relaxed and open minded, the decision simply appears (*it just popped into my mind!*).

286

Don't push. While you're keeping your head down and working really hard, you might miss something important. Instead, lift your head up, and practice being observant and open to receiving.

Instead of struggling to arrive at a decision, wait for the decision to arrive at your doorstep.

Now, make that final plea to your Jury...
Feel this story's truth. Clear your mind, and breathe deeply. Now ask yourself: *What kind of person do I intend to be right now? What do I need to do to feel proud of myself when I'm done?*

Continue breathing deeply — Make a decision — Act!

*Back to **Making decisions** (page 275)*

Managing anger

Pivot away from frustration and anger, and into a relaxed focus on getting what you want.

Pivot Inspirations:

- *No harm, no foul* (page 290)

- *The stream flows around the rocks* (page 293)

No harm, no foul

As is the case with many sports, basketball designates a few people—referees—to enforce the rules of the game by calling fouls. As much as players may at times disagree with the referees, it's really helpful to have them there. It allows the two teams to focus on *playing the game* instead of *policing it*.

Still, not all games are organized; many are informal. So called *pickup games* happen in school yards, streets, parks, back yards, and recreational centers. During pickup games, it's up to individual players to call fouls when they happen.

Now, if you've ever seen a basketball game in which the referees call many fouls, you'll understand how *boring* that can be. Every time a foul is called during an organized game, play stops, and either the ball needs to be thrown back in from out of bounds or a player gets to shoot free throws. In either case, it slows the game down, making it far less exciting and interesting. If referees call too many fouls, the crowd may start to boo them.

In pickup games, no one shoots free throws, but calling many fouls and frequently stopping play can be a real drag. It's possible that the game could be hijacked by an overly nitpicky perfectionist. Also, if you've got two nitpicky perfectionists who disagree, you risk a big fight.

To keep the game flowing nicely, players will remind each other from time to time, saying, *no harm, no foul!* I know that the term has found its way into popular culture, but let me explain what it means during pickup basketball games: it's a plea to let the little things go and just get on with enjoying the game.

If your shot missed the basket due more to you than to someone bumping you, then let it go. If the person's toe touched the end line while throwing the ball in bounds, let it go. If the person took one too many steps before shooting the ball, and if she disagrees with you calling "traveling," let it go.

Nothing's more important than the enjoyment of a game moving along at an enjoyable pace.

*   *   *

Where in the rest of our lives do we have the opportunity to whisper to ourselves, *no harm, no foul*, so we can continue without distractions or disruption? The *Forward* to this book applies *no harm, no foul* to calming anger while driving in difficult traffic. Perhaps it can be applied to an off-the-cuff remark by a friend or boss, being on the receiving end of minor bad manners, slightly less-than-perfect service delivery, or your partner uncharacteristically forgetting an anniversary.

When do small mistakes or infractions *have nothing to do*, really, with your overall goal?

Here are some lessons that are at the heart of *no harm, no foul*:

- Stop expecting perfection.

- Nobody's perfect, including me and you; if you give someone else a break, maybe you'll *get* a break in return.

- *Perfect is the enemy of "done."*

- Keep a focus on the big picture instead of minor details.

- Don't expect everything in life to be fair.

- Letting the little things go helps you to practice *resilience*, which is the ability to succeed in the face of difficulty.

- Become so skilled that even minor unfairness can't stop you.

- Life is a *marathon*, not a *sprint*; if unfairness prevented you from succeeding today, figure out how to work around it next time.

Now, make that final plea to your jury...

Feel this story's truth. Clear your mind, and breathe deeply. Now ask yourself: *What kind of person do I intend to be right now? What do I need to do to feel proud of myself when I'm done?*

Continue breathing deeply — Make a decision — Act!

Back to **Managing anger** (page 289)

The stream flows around the rocks

Defense Attorney's story for your Jury...
Different situations produce anger. For example, not getting what we want can piss us off. Feeling that a situation is wrong or unfair can be wildly frustrating. Anger can often be an emotion that we feel immediately after being hurt (*Oh, yeah? I'll hurt you as much as you just hurt me!*) or frightened (*Oh, yeah? The best defense is a good offense!*).

This story is about the particular anger felt when you can't get a person or situation to give you what you want. Think of it as you meeting an immovable object, which calls to mind the wise saying about the stream and the rock.

The moving water of a stream is powerful enough to push some objects along in its current. For example, a leaf, a feather, or bits of pollen are easily carried downstream. The water meets the object and moves it.

When water encounters a large rock, however, it can't move it or flow through it. Water can't "see the situation coming" and reroute itself ahead of time, thereby avoiding the conflict. Instead, the water needs to move right up against the rock before naturally *flowing around it*. It surges to the left, to the right, or over the top. The water naturally finds the path of least resistance and *keeps going*.

Now, it can get really interesting if you observe this principle over very long periods of time. In the long run, water can actually wear down and reduce the size of rock. So on the one hand, flowing around the rock often enough can eventually eliminate it. On the other hand, *no one has* **time** *for all that!* The stream has its natural job to do—*to keep flowing.*

Spend more time concentrating on how to keep flowing and less time focusing on why the rock won't move for you.

*   *   *

Your life is *important*, and there's a *flow* to it. When you encounter a person or situation that isn't giving you what you want, cascade or surge around it. Try moving to the left. If it blocks you in that direction, see if you can flow to the right or flow over it. There's almost always a way to get around it so you can keep moving, keep flowing.

Getting what you want is the point, not necessarily getting it from *this particular situation.* Flow around it, move on, and find another way to get what you want further downstream.

Now, make that final plea to your Jury...
Feel this story's truth. Clear your mind, and breathe deeply. Now ask yourself: *What kind of person do I intend to be right now? What do I need to do to feel proud of myself when I'm done?*

Continue breathing deeply — Make a decision — Act!
Back to **Managing anger** (page 289)

Reducing jealousy

Pivot away from jealousy, and into feeling secure in the presence of other impressive people.

Pivot Inspiration:

- *Be like the Beatles* (page 296)

Be like the Beatles

When coming of age in the 70s, I was a big-time Beatles fan even though the group had disbanded years earlier. I loved their energy, the four intriguing and distinct personalities, and the creativity of their music. You can cut off a song in the middle, pretend to be a band with a different name, play instruments from other cultures, and string together six songs uninterrupted by any silence in between? *Whoa!*

More than 40 years after breaking up, their music and song writing are considered to be some of the most masterful, impressive, and popular of the twentieth century.

Given the accolades and adoration heaped upon them over time, one might wonder how such a wildly talented group came to be in the first place. I'd be happy to share, here, my best understanding of how the members met and how the group evolved.

While in their mid-teens, Paul McCartney met the several-years-older John Lennon after a performance by John's band, The Quarrymen. Paul's personality was far less rough-and-tumble, but he could play a few more chords on the guitar. Putting aside personality differences, John decided to make the group stronger by inviting Paul to join.

Paul had a friend and schoolmate named George Harrison and bragged that George could play more chords than either him or John. As the story goes, the three met on a bus, and the boys encouraged George to do an impromptu audition for John right then and there. Although the then 17-year-old John was concerned about George being too young at 14 years of age, he decided to invite him to join the band.

Four years later, the Beatles were friendly with a very popular drummer named Ringo Starr, who at that time played for the band, Rory Storm and the Hurricanes. Although I'm not aware of the details, it was decided that the group would be stronger—both musically and in popularity—if they fired their current drummer and brought Ringo into the band.

Consistently, when John and the other Beatles encountered someone with more talent, a different skill, or more popularity, they included the person instead of jealously rejecting him. It wasn't always easy to do. Paul was better looking than John, and John was smarter and cooler than Paul. George could play guitar better than all of them, and Ringo was by far the most popular. Nonetheless, there was a mutual understanding that they were far more powerful together than they were apart.

This extended to their friendships and musical collaborations as well. The Beatles were drawn to and befriended gifted people such as Bob Dylan and Eric Clapton.

Instead of perceiving others as threats, they brought more talented people into the fold and made their group stronger. And stronger. *And stronger yet!*

*   *   *

Granted, most of us probably are not destined to make musical history. Nevertheless, all of us learn and develop by surrounding ourselves with more talented people. When a group gets stronger, we can reap huge individual benefits.

Also, as long as we can define clear roles for people, helping them to work collaboratively instead of at cross purposes, then the group gets stronger with added talent. Remember that, if you can't find a way to include additional talent, someone else will. How many times in history have we seen someone pushed out of a group due to pettiness and jealousy, only to have that person leave and find wild success with a competing group?

What will be your next chance to put ego aside, leverage opportunity, and boost the effectiveness of your group? How will the increased power of the group come back around and help your individual learning, development, and success? Are you willing to risk finding out?

Are you willing to take the chance needed to play for the Beatles, or would you rather be the star of a band no one's ever heard of?

Now, make that final plea to your Jury...

Feel this story's truth. Clear your mind, and breathe deeply. Now ask yourself: *What kind of person do I intend to be right now? What do I need to do to feel proud of myself when I'm done?*

Continue breathing deeply — Make a decision — Act!

Back to **Reducing jealousy** (page 295)

Relaxing about mistakes

Pivot away from fear of mistakes and failure, and into calmly learning from them.

Pivot Inspirations:

- *Don't get heavy, unless...* (page 300)

- *Don't use a hammer to flip an egg* (page 303)

- *Highway rumble strips* (page 306)

- *Miniature golf (putt-putt)* (page 310)

Don't get heavy, unless...

Defense Attorney's story for your Jury...

I've developed a good amount of experience providing counseling for people who at first either didn't want it or weren't sure. I've done court ordered substance abuse counseling, couples counseling in which one partner wanted me to "fix" the other, and work with kids whose parents wanted me to "get them to behave."

With time and practice, I found ways to make these types of situations enjoyable and productive for everyone involved. In particular, I really like working with middle-school-aged and teen-aged children, and I thought I'd share a technique of mine that works quite well with these young adults.

After establishing as much confidentiality as possible, my next job is to reassure the teen that I'm not another heavy authority figure who's there to lecture and shame them. To accomplish this, I cut a deal:

> *Unless you're describing a situation that involves death, losing a limb, getting an incurable disease, creating a baby you can't care for, becoming instantly homelessness, getting raped, or getting tossed into jail on a serious charge, I promise not to get heavy and intense with you. With all other topics, we'll explore your options, and I'll give you space to decide how you'd like to handle things. Deal?*

They always accept. It sounds—*and **is**—*so reasonable.

This accomplishes several goals. First, my teenage client relaxes and opens up about delicate topics, allowing me to be a consultant who helps her to think through options and to make better decisions, instead of barging in as someone interested only in barking orders or judging.

Second, I accomplish a sneakier goal. Most teenagers are not skilled at understanding the consequences of their actions, so they inadvertently wander into topics (for example, going to a big party on Saturday night) that actually involve some serious danger (drinking and using drugs, which make them vulnerable to rape or a DUI or a car accident). When I gently help them to make the connection to potential danger, they're more willing to hear me and heed my advice.

*　　*　　*

If hearing this story helps you to be a more skilled consultant to teenagers in your life, that would be great. Though I'm hoping you'll see an adult application as well.

As this book mentioned in previous chapters, fear distorts your perception of reality, limits your creativity, invites procrastination and avoidance, and drains your energy. If the fear is irrational, you can lessen it by moving carefully toward and *then through it*, despite how intimidating this might feel at the time.

In my coaching sessions, I routinely hear adult clients freaking out about all sorts of trivial things: whether the hot girl will want to go out on a second date, whether the good student will get into her preferred college, whether he's too fat, whether a friend is talking trash behind his back, or whether she'll interview well enough to get the job.

The next time stress, anxiety, or some other kind of irrational or over-the-top fear threatens to shut down effective action, make the same deal with yourself that I do with teenagers. If this imagined bad thing happens, will it kill you or someone else, lop off a limb, make you instantly homeless? Will it give you an incurable disease or get you thrown in jail for a felony?

If not, *then relax!* There's room and time for some trial and error, for making mistakes, and for figuring things out. Remember that *Nervous You* is not nearly as skilled and capable as *Calm You*. Calm You is more likely to get the job done and get you what you want. Save the freak out for the truly threatening situations.

Now, make that final plea to your Jury...
Feel this story's truth. Clear your mind, and breathe deeply. Now ask yourself: *What kind of person do I intend to be right now? What do I need to do to feel proud of myself when I'm done?*

Continue breathing deeply — Make a decision — Act!

Back to **Relaxing about mistakes** (page 299)

Don't use a hammer to flip an egg

Defense Attorney's story for your Jury...
To get something done, you need the right tools. Beyond that, if you have the most modern, *helpful* tools, it can increase the likelihood of your success, and the odds of you getting it done as quickly and easily as possible.

Of course, different tasks require different tools. For example, chefs, poets, carpenters, and graphic designers all need different tools. Even when looking at one general type of task, such as cooking, there are still different needs for tools; a pastry chef would use a somewhat different set of tools than a short order cook at a diner, and a candy maker uses different tools than someone barbecuing in the back yard.

When trying to accomplish goals, my Life & Career Coaching clients sometimes try approaches that don't work, and they draw some unfortunate conclusions. For example, they might assume that they're stupid or incapable of getting the job done. Or perhaps their mind goes to the idea that achieving their goal is impossible, hopeless.

Many times, my clients are not only smart, strong, and capable enough to get the job done, but they are using a perfectly good tool *in an incredibly* **wrong** *way.*

Consider for a moment what it would be like to have a tool belt with only one tool: a hammer. Of course, a hammer is great for hammering and removing nails, and you can use it for some odd tasks (for example, breaking one large block of frozen-together ice cubes). Yet, as useful as a hammer can be, it's limited. If you need to insert a screw, paint a wall, apply spackle, or take a measurement, the hammer is either incredibly awkward or useless. Use a hammer to flip an egg? You make a big mess!

Now, here's the most important part. When you make a mess by using a hammer to flip an egg, trim a rose bush, write a poem, or clean your windshield, the resulting mess *is not the hammer's fault.* It's also not the fault of the person who had only that one tool with which to work. It's the fault of the supervisor who provided only the hammer.

So, get your supervisor to select a more appropriate tool for your worker, and watch your results improve.

*   *   *

Here are some common approaches that prove to be wonderful tools in some situations and "a big part of the problem" at other times:

- Being gentle and comforting

- Being firm

- Working harder

- Taking a break

- Confronting a situation

- Ignoring a situation

- Relying on logic

- Relying on feelings

- Relying on what other people think

- Relying only on your opinion

Given that we are creatures of habit, we may over rely on one tool and wildly neglect using another. The more tools you can place in your tool belt—or utensils you can keep in your kitchen, or time management tools you can use at work—the better. With that increased flexibility, when one tool fails, you can try a few others.

Now, make that final plea to your Jury...
Feel this story's truth. Clear your mind, and breathe deeply. Now ask yourself: *What kind of person do I intend to be right now? What do I need to do to feel proud of myself when I'm done?*

Continue breathing deeply — Make a decision — Act!

*Back to **Relaxing about mistakes*** (page 299)

Highway rumble strips

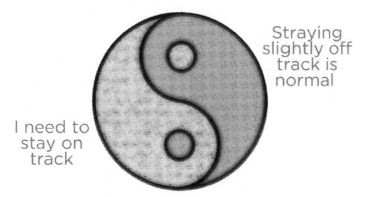

Straying slightly off track is normal

I need to stay on track

For the vast majority of us, if I asked you to drive a route from your home to another familiar location—the supermarket, work, a friend's house—it would be no problem, right?

You know the route, most of your driving is easy and automatic, and you obey the traffic laws along the way. You always feel confident about arriving at your destination, and feel reasonably safe and secure while doing it.

Yet, did you realize that you were off course almost the entire way? *Yep*, you were! I know you don't believe me, but let me explain further.

First, no one drives in a straight line from one destination to another. If you look at your route on a map, there would be zigs and zags. Literally, for most of your drive, the front of your car was *almost never* directly pointed at the exact destination.

Second, the next time you're in the front passenger seat, notice how often the car isn't perfectly aligned within its lane. The car drifts right, it comes close to the line, and the driver notices and adjusts back toward the middle. It drifts in the other direction, and the driver realigns the car's path again. The road curves quickly or unexpectedly, and the car could be pointing way off the road. The driver slows and adjusts, and the car aligns within the curving lane. Again, the car spends almost no time perfectly positioned in the middle of the lane.

Change. *Adjust.* Change. *Adjust.* Repeat often.

Clearly, *being off track* is a natural part of *being **on** track*. Having said that, how can we tell when getting off track has gone too far? When is it time to push the panic button? To understand the difference between the need for a slight adjustment as opposed to addressing an emergency, let me tell you a story....

Imagine that you're driving in the slow lane of a highway. Your car begins to drift, but you're too busy chatting with your passengers to notice. In this case, you're failing to  adjust so that the car stays in the lane.

At this point, my story will become absurd, but I do so to illustrate what it takes to make a really big mess.

Now imagine that the car hits the rumble strips in the breakdown lane, but the driver ignores it. *Problem? What problem?!*

Next, the car is driving on the grass next to the highway. *Quit freaking out, you worry too much!*

Now, the car is headed down an embankment. *We'll be OK. We're in an SUV.* At this point, it enters an open field. *I'll fix this situation, but just give me a few minutes to get to it.* Somehow, the car has managed to enter the woods without hitting the first couple of trees. *It's OK...I've got great insurance.* Finally, the car smashes into a rock or tree. *Darn! OK...OK...I messed up.*

At this point, a slight tug at the steering wheel won't fix the situation; you're going to have to call a tow truck, drag the car out of the woods and into a repair shop, get the car fixed, pay potential legal fines for damages incurred during your misadventure, and work toward getting back onto the road over time.

Getting off track doesn't create a big mess. *Failing to get back on track quickly* causes the mess.

So, don't panic when your car touches the edge of the lane; just make a simple adjustment. If you happen to experience the rumble strips or grass, take it very seriously, and make a quick and significant course correction. Follow these guidelines, and you should have a very safe and successful journey.

Our goal should be to live happy, healthy, and fruitful lives. It shouldn't be about becoming some kind of Perfection Robot, and it shouldn't be lived in denial.

When are we overreacting to everyday mistakes that need only slight adjustment, and when are we ignoring so many mistakes that we're about to crash and burn? The sweet spot is in the middle, when you're paying attention to detail and doing your best in the moment.

Now, make that final plea to your Jury...
Feel this story's truth. Clear your mind, and breathe deeply. Now ask yourself: *What kind of person do I intend to be right now? What do I need to do to feel proud of myself when I'm done?*

Continue breathing deeply — Make a decision — Act!

*Back to **Relaxing about mistakes** (page 299)*

Miniature golf (putt-putt)

Let's say you decided to take some time off and treat yourself to a relaxing game of miniature golf (putt-putt). The goal is to spend time outdoors, enjoy, unwind, and relax.

Now on the one hand, there's no pressing need to keep score or to try to "do well." You're alone, so you have no one to impress or please except yourself. There's no competition going on. There's no prize money or trophy, so there's nothing important at stake. It's just you, the course, and the beautiful spring day.

On the other hand, instead of just whacking the ball without a care, it's more fun to challenge yourself to do well. The best way to do that is to keep score, try to make or beat par for each hole, or try to beat your total score from the last time you played. Measuring your progress and striving to get better makes the game more interesting and fun, right?

Now, off you go onto the course. When you hit the ball with force and it bounces off the putting green, you smile and think, *OK, try tapping it.* You tap the ball next time, and you find that it still moves too fast and out of control. You think, *Try to strike through the ball smoothly.*

Each time you try something that doesn't work, it energizes you, gets your mind thinking, and stokes your curiosity for finding another way to do it. You focus the same way when facing other challenges on the course: ramps, the windmill, a tunnel. If it takes three or four attempts before you find a way that works, no big deal! It's fun to figure things out, right?

By staying focused on how much fun it is to try new things, you relax, concentrate, stay curious, and are flexible and open to experimentation. With this relaxed, fun approach, improvement happens and your skill level rises.

At this point, let's switch things up a bit. The top goals are not to relax, challenge yourself playfully, and have fun. Remember that the top goal is to *do well*, and it's *important* that that happen, darn it.

With this new priority and approach, the first thing that happens is that your ability to blend relaxation and concentration disappears. You're tight and nervous before you begin, concentrating to the point of stressing yourself out.

The next thing that happens is that each mistake brings you closer and closer to the line of Making Too Many Mistakes. If you make mistakes on two holes in a row, then **you can't make a mistake on this next hole**, otherwise you'll need several "holes in one" to make up for it!!! The task gets harder and harder as you go, and each hole becomes more and more intense.

In this state, when you make a mistake, others might be noticing you sweating, swearing, throwing your club, screaming, crying, threatening to give up, or acting helpless so someone will come to rescue you. Face it, you'd be a hot mess. *Attention! Meltdown on hole number 9.*

*   *   *

OK, now let's come back to reality. *NOBODY* plays putt-putt like that, becoming a freak show over minor mistakes. It would be absurd, right? Yet, how often do we approach other tasks in our lives—housekeeping, school assignments, work projects, dinner parties, raising our children—in the same way as the Maniac on Hole 9?

Before wrapping up this story, skim it again, and notice that the word "mistake" never appears in the relaxed version of the story, and notice that just about every sentence in the uptight version mentions "mistake." A huge part of the problem is too much attention paid to avoiding mistakes and not enough paid to generating *creative solutions.*

When you focus on fun, learning, curiosity, and improving, then your efforts produce much better results. When you focus on "not making a mistake," you tend to make more mistakes. Even if you can maniacally drive yourself to avoid mistakes, you'll make yourself and those around you miserable, hammer your nervous system with too much stress, and cut yourself off from your best creativity. Human beings need to *be relaxed* in order to be at their creative best.

So the next time you put pressure on yourself not to make mistakes, think instead about playing putt-putt, relax as if you're alone on that miniature golf course on a warm spring day, and strive to learn and improve because *it's **more fun** to play that way*. See each effort as an opportunity to learn how to do it better *next time*, and enjoy the process of improvement over time. You'll get much better, much quicker that way.

Now, make that final plea to your Jury...

Feel this story's truth. Clear your mind, and breathe deeply. Now ask yourself: *What kind of person do I intend to be right now? What do I need to do to feel proud of myself when I'm done?*

Continue breathing deeply — Make a decision — Act!

*Back to **Relaxing about mistakes*** (page 299)

Taking better care of yourself

Pivot away from rushing or pleasing others, and into loving self-care.

Pivot Inspirations:

- *Airplane oxygen mask (page 316)*

- *Eat before you go food shopping (page 318)*

- *Fill your fridge (page 320)*

- *Leave their opinions on the porch (page 323)*

- *Take a lifesaver ring with you (page 326)*

- *Wear your armor (page 329)*

Airplane oxygen mask

Defense Attorney's story for your Jury...
I remember as a teenager taking my first airplane flight. I'd been very involved in Boy Scouts and was invited to participate in a Jamaican Jamboree (a camping trip). I'd first need to catch a flight to Miami, stay there overnight, and then continue on to the Caribbean island. Quite the initial airplane trip!

One small detail stands out for me in that early experience. I recall being very surprised when the airline attendant explained the use of the oxygen masks.

The attendant said that, should the cabin pressure drop, oxygen masks will fall from overhead compartments. She said, *Put the mask on yourself before assisting a child or elderly traveling companion.*

Being the good Boy Scout that I was, I thought that doing good deeds and helping other people were important. When I first heard these instructions, they sounded selfish. Why shouldn't we be helping the less able before helping ourselves? These instructions felt wrong to me.

Then, someone explained the logic. Emergencies can be harried and chaotic. If I'm fumbling to put a mask onto a struggling companion, and if I pass out from lack of oxygen before helping that person, then the two of us might die. By putting on my mask first, I'm getting what I need first, so I'm then fully able to help others.

Most caregiver situations are not as intense as an airplane emergency, though the basic principle applies to everyday situations as well. For example, it's easier to feed others when you're not horribly hungry yourself. If you're well rested, you'll have the attention span and energy to provide excellent care to those in your charge.

Finally, one of the ways in which young people develop is to observe others as a way to learn. In this situation, we say that the observed person is *modeling good behavior* for others. By making sure that you "put your mask on first," you're highlighting the importance of self-love and self-care, which is a critical lesson to teach children.

Now, make that final plea to your Jury...

Feel this story's truth. Clear your mind, and breathe deeply. Now ask yourself: *What kind of person do I intend to be right now? What do I need to do to feel proud of myself when I'm done?*

Continue breathing deeply — Make a decision — Act!

Back to **Taking better care of yourself** (page 315)

Eat before you go food shopping

Defense Attorney's story for your Jury...
Many of us have had the challenging and unfortunate experience of going grocery shopping when we are very, *very* hungry. The result isn't pretty.

Because your ravenous body is screaming, everything in the supermarket looks good, especially fast and junky food. Without really thinking about it, items seem to find their way into your shopping cart.

When you arrive home after shopping, you'll discover a good amount of sugary and fatty food in your grocery bags. There may be huge chocolate bars, comfort food from your childhood (a bit too much mac and cheese or shepherd's pie), salty and crunchy snacks, cakes and ice creams, artificial dairy cream topping, or way too many cookies with that unnaturally colored, holiday-themed filling (*but they looked so **festive!***).

After over spending, buying too many, and eating too much, it's tempting to turn on yourself with criticism. *Why did I buy all that stuff? Why did I eat it? What's **wrong** with me?*

Well...*nothing's* wrong with you. You were set up. You were deprived and then blamed for acting like a deprived person. Put vulnerable people into a wildly tempting situation, and the result is just about a foregone conclusion.

In order to get better results next time, be *nicer* to yourself. Prepare yourself properly. In the same way that you put gas in the car before you expect to take it on a long drive, *feed yourself* before running errands, even if it's just a healthy, quick snack to hold you over until you can eat a full meal.

It's the kind and decent thing to do, isn't it?

*   *   *

In what other areas of our lives are we "food shopping while hungry"? Perhaps going into a meeting unprepared, saying yes when you needed to say no, or ignoring dating red flags because of intense loneliness. How can we "feed ourselves first" to avoid those situations?

Now, make that final plea to your Jury...
Feel this story's truth. Clear your mind, and breathe deeply. Now ask yourself: *What kind of person do I intend to be right now? What do I need to do to feel proud of myself when I'm done?*

Continue breathing deeply — Make a decision — Act!

*Back to **Taking better care of yourself** (page 315)*

Fill your fridge

Defense Attorney's story for your Jury...
In today's busy, modern life, it can be a challenge to eat in a healthy way. One specific challenge is preparing meals at home and not over relying on restaurants.

Many of us know what it's like at the end of a particularly grueling day at work, toying with the idea of using the drive-through window, ordering take-out, hitting a restaurant, or having a pizza delivered to the house. Some of it is "emotional eating": eating comforting food—often sugary or fatty foods—when feeling emotionally down or upset. Yet some of it can simply be physical weariness from the work and commute, and struggling to find energy on an empty stomach.

Let's say that you've burned some willpower to make it home without going through the fast-food drive-through window. You've convinced yourself that you're going to be good and that you're going to prepare a healthy meal for dinner. Then when you arrive home and check the refrigerator and cabinets, you realize that you haven't gone shopping for a long time. *The fridge and cupboards are practically bare!*

After grabbing the menu for Chinese takeout or darting out the door on your way to the neighborhood pub, you might feel tempted to turn on yourself with criticism. *Why didn't you make do with the food I had in the house? Why did I order all that fattening food at the restaurant? What's* **wrong** *with me?*

Well, *nothing's* wrong with you! You were set up. You were deprived and then blamed for acting like a deprived person.

Put vulnerable people into a wildly tempting situation, and the result is just about a foregone conclusion.

In order to get better results next time, be *nicer* to yourself. Fill your fridge and cupboards weekly. Keep healthy snacks easily available, so you'll have the energy needed to prepare a proper meal. Prepare some meals ahead of time, so you allow yourself some "grab, microwave, and go" food.

It's the kind and decent thing to do, isn't it?

*   *   *

What are other instances in which we fail to prepare and then blame ourselves for acting like an unprepared person? In what other instances are we not "filling our fridges"? Perhaps when we are:

- Procrastinating

- Not asking for help

- Rushing

- Pushing through without taking adequate breaks

- Not moving our bodies enough, being too sedentary

- Expecting excellent physical performance without warming up, not working your way up to it gradually

- Not rehearsing before being interviewed or giving a presentation

In these instances, think of preparation as an act of love. When you love someone, you've "got their back," right? So, don't let your loved one go into a situation unprepared.

Now, make that final plea to your Jury...
Feel this story's truth. Clear your mind, and breathe deeply. Now ask yourself: *What kind of person do I intend to be right now? What do I need to do to feel proud of myself when I'm done?*

Continue breathing deeply — Make a decision — Act!

*Back to **Taking better care of yourself*** (page 315)

Leave their opinions on the porch

One of the most *practical* architectural inventions has to have been the mud room. I can still hear my mother all those years ago yelling as we entered the back door after playing outside: *Don't track that in here!* She knew that we were covered in *something*. It could be snow, mud, dirt, paint...whatever it was on that day, she didn't want it messing up her house.

In our tiny home, the back hallway was our mud room. It was there that we took off our coats and shoes, and it's where we left our sporting equipment. Our washer and drier were located adjacent to the hallway, so it was easy to put dirty clothes directly into the washer before entering the house.

Later, after items had dried, we could brush them off, toss them into the washer, take them outside for scraping or banging, and sweep the floor of the hallway after everything else was clean.

It was about *containment*. Keep the mess right next to the door, and allow only clean bodies, clothes, and other items into the house.

Many of my clients struggle when dealing with the critical opinions of others, especially judgments coming from family members, loved ones, or bosses. Some of my clients automatically take these comments to heart, accepting them quickly and completely, allowing them all the way inside emotionally where they often create doubt, guilt, insecurity, fury, and other forms of suffering.

When managing this situation, many people bounce between two extreme and unhelpful approaches: ignoring feedback from others or taking everything to heart.

Instead, my suggestion is to take someone else's opinion, and leave it in your psychological mud room or out on the porch. Then over time, you can assess it, clean it, discard it, or bring it into your emotional house. On the one hand, you've received the comment: *there it is, right there on the porch.* However, you didn't bring it all the way in before feeling confident that it wouldn't create a big mess; you made sure that it would help and not hurt.

To offer another example, let's say someone brought you a used couch. Thank the person, and have them leave it on the porch. Tell them that you'll bring it in later. After the person leaves, inspect it. If the couch has bedbugs in it, you'll want to remove it from the porch and take it right out to the curb with the rest of the trash. Or, maybe it just needs little bit of cleaning before you place it in your home. Finally, it might be a helpful, perfect fit as is, and you can bring it right into the house.

Whichever way it plays out, it's *your choice*. **You are** in control, *not* the person who presented you with the "gift" of their opinion.

Now, make that final plea to your Jury...
Feel this story's truth. Clear your mind, and breathe deeply. Now ask yourself: *What kind of person do I intend to be right now? What do I need to do to feel proud of myself when I'm done?*

Continue breathing deeply — Make a decision — Act!

*Back to **Taking better care of yourself** (page 315)*

Take a lifesaver ring with you

Many years ago, when I was taking lifesaving classes at my Boy Scout camp, they gave us a shorthand mnemonic designed to recall the order of a water rescue: *Reach, Throw, Row,* and *Go.*

First, see if you can remain securely out of the water while reaching for the drowning person, pulling him or her to safety. Second, throw a floating device, such as a lifesaving ring, to the drowning  person. Third, if you can row a boat to the drowning person, allowing him to hold onto the side without you entering the water, do that. Fourth and finally, jump into the water, swim to the person, place the person's back on your hip, and sidestroke the person to safety. The idea was to avoid the last method, because there's a risk that the drowning person could pull you under, and both people could drown.

I'm reminded of this when my Life & Career Coaching clients talk about socially or emotionally overwhelming situations. It could be what we now call a Toxic Relationship or Environment. It might be a negative, whining, or needy partner or relative. Maybe it's a committee or group that demands more from you than you're willing or able to give. Possibly, it can be a manager at work who micromanages or changes expectations based on his mood, or it could be a dysfunctional family or team. Perhaps it's a neighbor who's always angry and confrontational.

Sometimes, it isn't the situation that's dysfunctional or toxic. It could be that you're involved with someone who needs more than you can give at that time. Such situations could involve childcare; caring for a physically, mentally, or emotionally dependent person; or caring for the elderly. Perhaps your work demands that you provide this level of intense care-taking.

These situations can sometimes threaten to overwhelm you, drown you. All the same, your values and principles demand that you relate, empathize, stay engaged, and assist; walking away altogether it not an option right now. *So...what do you do?*

When you enter into very demanding relational and social situations, don't jump into those emotional waters without having a way to make it back to shore. Don't put yourself in danger without protecting yourself. Assist others in a way in which you won't lose yourself.

To help in this way, imagine grabbing two lifesaver rings before entering their turbulent waters. One ring is for you to give to the troubled person or group to hold onto, which is your attempt to help them. The second one is for you, and it's tethered with a rope to the dock or shore. Your ring allows you to immerse yourself into their troubled waters—to be fully present with them, empathic and involved—without any threat of being pulled under or not being able to get back to safety.

If the person allows you to use the rope attached to their ring to pull them to safety, great! If they want or need to hang out in those troubled waters, floating on the ring you brought them, that's great as well! Your health, wellbeing, and safety are not dependent on whether you can save them. In this way, you can assist people in need—dealing with your boss, elderly mother, disabled brother, child, husband, therapy clients, condo board, or angry neighbor—without feeling overwhelmed, going under, or losing yourself to their situation.

Now, make that final plea to your Jury...

Feel this story's truth. Clear your mind, and breathe deeply. Now ask yourself: *What kind of person do I intend to be right now? What do I need to do to feel proud of myself when I'm done?*

Continue breathing deeply — Make a decision — Act!

*Back to **Taking better care of yourself*** (page 315)

Wear your armor

Defense Attorney's story for your Jury...

My Life & Career Coaching clients sometimes talk about socially or emotionally overwhelming situations. It could be what we now call a Toxic Relationship or Environment. It might be a negative, whining, or needy partner or relative. Maybe it's a committee or group that demands more from you than you're willing or able to give. Possibly, it can be a manager at work who micromanages or changes expectations based on his mood, or it could be a dysfunctional family or team. Perhaps it's a neighbor who's always angry and confrontational.

Sometimes, it isn't that the situation is dysfunctional or toxic. It could be that you're involved with someone who needs more than you can give at that time. Such situations could involve childcare; caring for a physically, mentally, or emotionally dependent person; or caring for the elderly. Perhaps your work demands that you provide this level of intense care-taking.

These situations can sometimes threaten to break your heart, to hurt you very deeply. All the same, your values and principles demand that you relate, empathize, stay engaged, and assist; walking away altogether it not an option right now. *So...what do you do?*

Try this....

Imagine yourself wearing medieval armor, with a metal breastplate and no helmet. Understand deeply and fully that

329

your most vulnerable parts are protected, especially your heart.

Now as you deal with your boss, elderly mother, disabled brother, child, husband, therapy clients, condo board, or angry neighbor, give them your head, but do not surrender your heart. Keep it protected behind the armor.

In that way, you can be fully present with them—paying them respectful and deep attention, being empathic and involved—without any emotional threat coming from their thrashing and messiness. Hear, think about, and respond with your head, coolly and rationally. Use your face to show them that you *understand how they feel*, but don't expose your heart to *feeling it fully* (it's **their** emotional situation, *not yours*).

After you leave their presence, remove your armor, and let your heart fully engage with the world again.

Now, make that final plea to your Jury...
Feel this story's truth. Clear your mind, and breathe deeply. Now ask yourself: *What kind of person do I intend to be right now? What do I need to do to feel proud of myself when I'm done?*

Continue breathing deeply — Make a decision — Act!

*Back to **Taking better care of yourself** (page 315)*

Trying something different

Pivot away from frustration and anxiety, and into open mindedness.

Pivot Inspirations:

- *Chinese finger trap* (page 332)

- *Pull the door, don't push it* (page 334)

- *Replace that bad habit* (page 336)

Chinese finger trap

Have you ever played with a Chinese finger trap? It's a sheath often made of woven bamboo that fits on the fingers. The forefingers of both hands are placed in either end of a single trap, as shown in this picture:

Our instinct is to pull our fingers out the ends of the sheath, away from each other. Yet, as we pull away, the weave tightens, making it impossible to escape the trap without breaking the bamboo.

The solution is to move your fingers toward each other, relaxing the weave, allowing your fingers to slip out the holes on either end.

*   *   *

This ancient game offers several bits of wisdom:

- Sometimes the solution is the opposite of what we first assumed would work.

- Slowing down and relaxing often produce better results that hurrying or tightening up.

- Sometimes "trying harder" won't work; it may even be part of the problem.

- If what you're doing isn't working, try something different.

The definition of insanity is doing the same thing over and over, often harder and faster, and expecting different results.

Now, make that final plea to your Jury...

Feel this story's truth. Clear your mind, and breathe deeply. Now ask yourself: *What kind of person do I intend to be right now? What do I need to do to feel proud of myself when I'm done?*

Continue breathing deeply — Make a decision — Act!

*Back to **Trying something different** (page 331)*

Pull the door, don't push it

Defense Attorney's story for your Jury...
It's happened to *all* of us throughout our lives, and I still fall into this trap from time to time.

As I'm having a conversation with someone—or daydreaming or stressing about my To-Do list or otherwise rushing about—I grab the door knob, twist, and push, but the door won't open. Still wrapped up in conversation or lost in thought, I twist and push again. *Nothing.*

Now, I'm irritated, perhaps a bit flustered. I twist and push again, *harder* this time. Still nothing! Is the door locked? Blocked on the other side? *Am I missing something?*

At this point, I slow down, surrender all preoccupations, and give the situation my full attention. *I'm going nowhere* until I figure this out.

More out of instinct than anything else, I now gently turn the nob and *pull.*

Boom! The door opens easily.

Red faced, shaking my head, I exit the room and get on with my day.

*   *   *

On the one hand, this is a fairly easy problem to solve. On the other hand, in what other areas of our lives are we heeding the instinct to go faster and harder in the same direction, when a different approach is what's needed?

Here are some bits of wisdom we all can take from the "pull the door open, don't push it" situation:

- Sometimes the solution is the opposite of what we first assumed would work.

- Slowing down and giving something your full attention leads to a better understanding of what's needed.

- Sometimes "trying harder" won't work; it may even be part of the problem.

- If what you're doing isn't working, try something different.

  The definition of insanity is doing the same thing over and over, often harder and faster, and expecting different results.

Now, make that final plea to your Jury...

Feel this story's truth. Clear your mind, and breathe deeply. Now ask yourself: *What kind of person do I intend to be right now? What do I need to do to feel proud of myself when I'm done?*

Continue breathing deeply — Make a decision — Act!

Back to **Trying something different** (page 331)

Replace that bad habit

Sometimes, it can be very difficult to motivate yourself to quit a bad habit *for your own* sake. Instead, you might feel more motivated to get the job done for the sake *someone you love*. This is a story of one of the most creative ways that a Life & Career Coaching client of mine leveraged his love of family to boost his motivation for change.

Years ago, I routinely provided hypnosis for people who wanted to quit smoking. As part of the treatment, before administering the hypnosis, I had a conversation with everyone about habit change.

In particular, I stressed that people who replaced smoking with another habit had more success than people who just wanted to eliminate the smoking. When you create a hole by removing the bad habit, something wants to flow in and take up that space; if you don't have something else to fill it, then smoking might creep back in. I also cautioned them about replacing smoking with lollipops and candy, which might cause weight gain.

I remember this one particular client because of his ingenuity. At the end of the last hypnosis session, I asked him how his habit replacement had been going. He told me that he'd kept an empty cigarette package, cut straws the size of cigarettes, and refilled the package with them. Then when he felt a craving to smoke, he pulled out his cigarette package—as he was habitually used to doing—and then he'd take a straw,

336

chew and finger it for a while, and toss the gnarled straw into the garbage.

To add some extra motivation, he took a picture of his young daughter, cut it to size, and placed it between the clear plastic wrap and the outside of the cigarette package. In that way, whenever he responded to a craving, he had a visual reminder of how he wanted to live long enough to see his daughter grow up, and quitting smoking was a part of that plan.

*   *   *

To replace a bad habit, identify the craving (the urge to smoke), the cue (needing a break, feeling tired or stressed), and the reward (a calming manual and oral ritual). Then, replace the old routine (take out your package of cigarettes, hold one, light it, and smoke it) with a new routine (take out your package of straws, see your daughter and remind yourself why you're doing this, hold a straw, and chew it).

The brilliance of this replacement is how much of the original routine remains in place, and the simple visual cue that grabbed his heart and focused him emotionally. For this man, love and family trumped his nicotine cravings.

So, get creative. Try different things. Knowing yourself as you do, find something simple and habitual that will kick up the emotion and motivation needed to do the right thing. What do you love, and how can you remind yourself that this habit change is the way you're going to get it?

Feel this story's truth. Clear your mind, and breathe deeply. Now ask yourself: *What kind of person do I intend to be right now? What do I need to do to feel proud of myself when I'm done?*

Continue breathing deeply — Make a decision — Act!

Back to **Trying something different** (page 331)

Appendix A: Let's look at mindfulness

Before you can use *Daily Pivots*, you first need to notice that you're being drawn into an unhelpful habit, hopefully recognizing the situation *right as it's beginning*.

Also, to pivot well, you need to know your *intention* in any given moment, to have an idea of the kind of man or woman you want to be, and to be clear about what kind of decision *that person* would make. Your intention is more of a *gut sense* than a *logical thought*.

The best way to improve these skills is to develop a daily **mindfulness practice**. Mindfulness has many benefits, including but not limited to observing yourself as you go about your active life, reducing stress, slowing your thinking, slowing your actions, appreciating the present moment, accepting challenging situations, and feeling calmer.

In very brief summary, mindfulness involves applying the techniques of meditation as you live your active, modern life. One great thing about practicing mindfulness is that you don't have to set aside time to do it; simply apply the techniques to what you're already doing. Great opportunities to practice mindfulness include taking a walk, having something to eat, driving, taking a shower, brushing your hair, taking your dogs for a walk, grooming your cat, or washing the dishes. For my clients struggling to find a time and place for mindfulness, I recommend that they do it every time they go to the bathroom, which is a very natural time for transition and for "taking a mental break" from the more intense pursuits of the day.

The exercises described in this appendix are based on the teachings of Marsha Linehan and the mindfulness techniques she presents in the Dialectical Behavioral Treatment (DBT) program.[49] I find her approach to be one of the easiest to grasp and apply.

Mindfulness exercises

I recommend that you do at least one mindfulness exercise daily, more if possible. An exercise lasts between 30 seconds and two minutes. You should see an increase in focus, more peace of mind, and less stress in your daily life sometime within a three- to four-month time period.

Select a singular activity (no multitasking) that you'll be doing alone, and apply mindfulness while doing it. To do so, take your attention and place it on what your five senses are experiencing—seeing, hearing, smelling, touching, tasting, which are sensations in your body—while you're active.

The process includes these three steps:

- Notice something sensual

- Think about what you're noticing

- Continue your activity without stopping

For example, you can notice an orange and yellow pitcher of lemonade sitting on the counter. You can think, I see the orange and yellow pitcher of lemonade...I see beads of sweat on the outside of the pitcher, and it's pooling around the base.

You can continue to wipe off the counter as you make this observation.

As another example, you can notice the leaves on the branches of a nearby tree as you're taking a walk. You can think, I see the leaves blowing in the tree. I'm feeling the breeze against my face as I walk. I smell freshly cut grass. I'm feeling my clothes move against me as I walk, and I'm noticing how hard and uneven the sidewalk feels as I plant my feet. As you make these observations, continue to walk without stopping.

Your observations can be as brief or as long as you like. For example, a perfectly valid thought about the pitcher of lemonade might be, Pitcher...lemonade...orange and yellow design...sweating...water on counter. If a thought about another topic enters your mind (I'm bored! What am I going to have for lunch?), gently notice it, and then return the focus to your bodily sensations without judging yourself or getting intense about it. It's OK if you have to redirect your attention many times during the few minutes you practice mindfulness, and this is especially true when you first begin this practice.

As you apply mindfulness, remember these principles to get the most out of the exercise:

- Do only one activity; *don't multitask!*

- Be like a reporter delivering facts without opinion, positive or negative.

- Do your task well and get the very most out of it.

So when you observe that pitcher of lemonade, avoid the urge to call it a "beautiful" or "ugly" pitcher. Avoid getting distracted by tangential thoughts, such as whether you prefer lemonade or iced tea. Don't analyze the situation and think about whether it's right or wrong that the pitcher is out on the counter and the possible identity of the person who might have failed to return the pitcher to the refrigerator. Just for a few minutes, keep your mind gently focused on only the facts that you can determine by seeing, hearing, smelling, tasting, or touching.

That's it! For 30 seconds up to a few minutes.

Do consider seeking a coach who can assist and improve your mindfulness practice.

Over time, you'll notice that you're able to stay present with the sensual experiencing for longer and longer periods, or that fewer or less intense thoughts interrupt your mindfulness practice. Like any skill, your ability gets stronger the more you practice.

Mindfulness teachers

There are many excellent mindfulness teachers and resources.

For example, the title of my professional blog is *Getting to Clear and Present* (http://gettingtoclearandpresent.blogspot.com), and it has a strong mindfulness focus. It shares techniques that I've tried, tells interesting stories, reviews helpful books on the subject, and more. For example, one blog posting documents *a very successful experiment of mine that involved weaving meditative techniques into my aerobic workouts at the gym*[50] (http://tinyurl.com/gym-meditation).

As for other mindfulness experiences and approaches, these teachers happen to be my favorites. Feel free to explore their books, websites, blogs, and other resources:

- **Dr. Marsha Linehan** is a psychiatrist, the founder of Behavioral Tech, LLC, and a developer of the Dialectical Behavioral Treatment (DBT) program. Mindfulness training is a key component of DBT, and the information in this appendix is strongly influenced by DBT.

- **Thich Nhat Hanh** is a Vietnamese Zen Buddhist Monk and a very highly regarded expert regarding mindfulness.

- **Joan Borysenko, PhD** is a best-selling author and speaker. Her book *Minding the Body, Mending the Mind* was one of the first that inspired me to incorporate mindfulness into the work that I do with clients.

- **Jon Kabat-Zinn, PhD** is a professor and author. In my opinion, Dr. Kabat-Zinn wins the prize for the coolest book title about applying mindfulness to modern life: *Full Catastrophe Living*.

Appendix B: Let's look at thinking habits

To pivot well, you need to be aware in a given moment of what you're doing and how you're feeling. You also need to have a calm, purposeful conversation with yourself that convinces you to avoid your unhelpful habit and pivot instead toward the change you want.

Rapid and intense thinking can prevent the awareness needed to pivot effectively. Also, if the thinking is particularly negative or rigid, it can kick up emotions and moods that, again, make it extremely difficult to focus enough to apply *Daily Pivots*.

In his classic book, *The Feeling Good Handbook*, David Burns describes ten patterns of thinking that are highly correlated with stress, depression, and anxiety.[51] I'll summarize a few key points in this appendix, but please do consider buying this incredibly helpful book.

THOUGHT STOPPING

Sometimes my clients tell me that they'd love to take my advice about healthier thinking habits, but their minds are racing too fast to allow them to practice. If you encounter this difficulty, I recommend that you begin your practice by experimenting with *thought stopping*. Sometimes the best thinking adjustment is just creating a brief moment of quiet.

Here are a few tips about how to interrupt rapid and intense thinking:

- Think *Shhhhh!* for a few seconds.

- Think *STOP!* in a loud, commanding voice.

- Picture a stop sign in your mind.

- Use hand lotion, and focus strongly on its scent and feel.

- Wear a rubber band on your wrist, and snap it when feeling speedy or upset; concentrate strongly on the sensation. (As a less harsh alternative, give your thigh a light pinch.)

These and other actions create a 1- to 2-second span of quiet in which to refocus on either mindfulness exercises or new thinking techniques.

Don't apply "mood gasoline"

The *How to "slip into a groove" without motivation* section in Chapter 3: Let's look at motivation describes the fleeting nature of an emotion or a feeling. In summary, an emotion flashes briefly through body and mind, usually as a response to an event or thought (it's triggered). Once your activity provides you with another different trigger, it's likely that you'll feel an emotion.

For example, you walk down the street and see a young couple in love: you feel warm, and you smile. Then, you hear a snippet of a song coming from a passing car that reminds you of an ex: now you feel bittersweet sadness.

Moods are emotions that intensify and linger over time. Think of what it means when someone says, He's in a mood! When moods linger for days or more, and if they seriously reduce your ability to do the daily tasks of living (self-care, parenting, household duties, work), they become diagnosable mood disorders.

The Feeling Good Handbook lists ten cognitive distortions, which I call mood gasoline. When you're feeling a difficult emotion and your thinking lapses into these patterns, it's like adding logs and gasoline to a small campfire, turning it into a bonfire or even a forest fire. The object is to catch yourself picking up the mood gasoline so you can put it back down again before someone gets hurt. Let the smaller campfire go out on its own.

Here are the cognitive distortions:[52]

- **All or nothing thinking**—You view a situation only in its most extremes. So, something is either awesome or horrible, or a person is either great or awful...nothing in between.

- **Overgeneralization**—When something bad happens, it's proof to you that it's always been that way and it will never change. *Here we go again...!*

- **Mental filter**—You focus on only the negatives and *don't even really see* the positives.

- **Discounting the positives**—If you happen to see a positive, *It doesn't count!*

347

- **Jumping to conclusions**—Either convincing yourself that you know what someone's thinking (*Oh, man, my boss has that look on his face...he must be mad at me*) or know what's going to happen in the future (*My boss is going to fire me, I know it!*).

- **Magnification or minimization**—You take a minor negative event and perceive it as being a big deal, or you take a big positive one and shrink it down until it means nothing.

- **Emotional reasoning**—If you feel something (*I feel like a loser!*), then it's true (*I **am** a loser!*). Or, when you come up with a story to explain the "logic" of something that's actually just a feeling; when you do this, the resulting story doesn't make much sense.

- **"Should" statements**—You add extra "verbal authority," saying *should, must, have to, ought to*, and so on.

- **Labeling or mislabeling**—You turn a mistake into a character trait and then call yourself names: *loser, idiot, fool, jerk*.

- **Personalization and blame**—If something bad happens, you take it personally and blame yourself inappropriately. Or, you blame others for things you did.

To avoid the cognitive distortions, detect these patterns in your thinking and speech, and switch to ones that don't allow the emotional campfire to grow out of control. Most of my clients like to think this through on-the-fly as they're going about their busy days. That being said, writing or typing the thought, labeling the distortion(s), and attempting to reword using more flexible, realistic language can add more power to the exercise.

Sometimes, the verbal switch is straight forward. For example, if you observe yourself thinking, *Oh, I should grab some lunch after I'm finished with this*, then you can reword it on-the-fly to this: *Hey, I just thought "should." How about, I'd **like** to have some lunch after I finish this.*

As a more involved example, here's a troubling thought: *What's the point of asking for a raise? It'll end up the same as all the other times I've ever asked for anything from her. I'm just a loser!* (The distortions in that statement are *overgeneralization* and *labeling*.)

You could try to rework the statement by saying something like this: *I haven't yet figured out how to ask my boss for a raise in a way that works. I suppose I could talk to a few coworkers I trust to see if they know of anything that works better. Also, maybe there are other ways I can learn how to "manage my manager." Failing that, it's time for me to start looking for another, better job.*

Most of the Pivot Inspiration stories are entertaining ways to move thinking away from cognitive distortions and toward more helpful, fun, relaxing, and hopeful perspectives. Here are a few additional methods that can help you avoid mood gasoline:

349

- Remind yourself that there's a lot you don't know. I'm acting as if I'm so sure of things—about myself, the future, others, life—but I really **don't know**. Keep an open mind.

- Get curious. Think of ways you can research the issue, get other opinions, or use trial-and-error to test some of your ideas.

- Concentrate on only the situation right in front of you in the present moment instead of dwelling on the past or future (to build this skill, see *Appendix A: Let's look at mindfulness*).

- Avoid evaluating situations using big-concept words such as justice, fair and unfair, appropriate, reasonable, respect, dignity, and so on. Instead, keep it simple. Focus on exactly what you want in observable and measurable terms (you can't really put a ruler up to justice or dignity), ask for exactly what you want, and dedicate yourself to learning how to get it over time and with practice...no excuses.

If you want to go right at some of the distortions directly, here are some guidelines:

- For all or nothing thinking, get in touch with how people, places, and things have a mix of good and bad attributes. List attributes that are neutral or different than the categories in which you'd been thinking. For example, if you'd been thinking that a concert is all bad or all good, you could note neutral, non-judgmental facts about it: for example, *musical, two hours long, held in a park, includes food venders*. Keep it simple by taking opinions, emotions, and criticisms out of the equation.

Another helpful method of breaking up this thinking is to create a weighted Pros and Cons list (see *The TTM stages of change* section in *Chapter 4: Let's look at change* for more information about creating this type of list).

- For overgeneralization, ask what you can do right now to make the situation better. I say to my Life & Career Coaching clients, play a psychological game with yourself, and pretend that there's no past and no future. For example, if you can't see or touch it right now, it doesn't exist. All that exists in the world is the situation right in front of you at this moment. How do you want to be about it? What do you choose to do with it?

- Also, you can purposefully focus on how this event is different than past, similar events, and you can fess up to what you did or didn't do that led to this situation using honest-but-compassionate language.

- For mental filter, focus on and list the positive and neutral parts of the situation.

- For discounting the positives, you could try discounting both the positives **and** negatives, because neither matter. What matters is for you to discover and use a course of action that will give you the effect you want. First, figure out the result you want from the situation. Then, what course of action is likely to get you what you want? Finally, how can you get started right in this moment with implementing your action plan? Be patient, use trial and error, and adjust your approach over time as you learn.

- For jumping to conclusions, remind yourself that *you don't know, really*. Also, you can ask the person what they're thinking, and then be sure to be a good sport about the fact that not everyone will be 100% honest when answering. Finally, instead of using all that guess work to evaluate a situation, you can focus on *what you want* instead (*I want my boss to think highly of me* or *I want to get a raise*) and all that you need to do to make it happen over time.

- For magnification or minimization, delay analysis, "sleep on it" for a while (if possible), and then refocus on what you prefer and how you can make it happen. Use a form of *It is what it is* that feels true to you, and avoid *It is what I **fear** it to be*.

- For emotional reasoning, state your feelings using emotion words: *happy, sad, worried, frustrated, angry*, and so on. Then, let it be, sit with it, and sleep on it. Practice separating *feelings* from *analysis*, and separating *feelings* from *actions*. Slow down, and ***just feel*** for a while.

Avoid saying *I feel* followed by logic, criticism, threat, or analysis: examples include *I feel like hurling a dish at your head* (instead, *I feel angry*), *I feel as if you're being unreasonable* (*I feel frustrated*), or *I feel like it's all going to go to hell in a handbasket* (*I feel worried*).

Try to use "I" statements. So, instead of saying, *You make me feel sad*, say *When you canceled our date, I felt sad*. The other person takes responsibility for *his actions*, and you take responsibility for *your feelings*.

- For "should" statements, use words that emphasize choice and desire: want to, choose to, decide to, and willing to. For example, I think things will turn out better for me if I decide to do that. I'll choose to do that. I want to do that.

- For labeling, pretend that you have a beloved friend who's feeling upset about a mistake, and coach the person to deal honestly with the situation without being so hard on himself. Again, remove the focus on character traits, and focus instead on learning from the mistake (everyone makes mistakes!) and correcting it.

- For personalization and blame, again, focus instead on learning from the situation and changing it, so that you get more of what you want. Instead of focusing too intensely on "what happened?", focus on what *you **want** to have happen **next time*** and how you can get that result over time.

If you think, *easier said than done*, then you're right! Think of this work in terms of *habit change*: you're in the habit of using cognitive distortions, and you'll need to practice new habits that include more flexible, manageable thinking.

Do consider seeking a coach who has expertise in "cognitive behavioral treatment (CBT)," and most importantly, who understands how to customize this material and make it fun. If all they can do is hand you a worksheet or workbook, find another coach.

To practice, flip the wording once in a given day, and it will have no overall effect. Yet, imagine doing it five or six times in a day, every day for a week, all month long, and for an entire year. Eventually, once you form your new, more-flexible thinking habits, it will feel as if you've taken an emotional backpack off your shoulders. Moving through life will feel lighter and more fun.

Practice, and give it time to become new thinking habits.

Hello! My name is Gerry Fisher, and I'm a unique Life & Career Coach who speeds up the time between dreaming and doing. Through writing, teaching, telling stories, and having conversations, I love to find the light switch inside everyone and help them *to turn it on.*

As an *emotion management expert,* I help my clients to overcome roadblocks to happiness and success. My background includes having produced *extraordinary results* as a licensed mental health counselor, assisting people with PTSD, panic attacks, depression, and more.

For example, a 26-year-old client once came to me averaging one psychiatric hospitalization **every month**; my work with her resulted in *TWO YEARS* without a hospitalization. If I can do that for someone with serious emotional disorders, imagine how I'd be able to help you pivot away from garden-variety procrastination, stress, worry, and blues toward *feeing at ease* while achieving your goals.

My Career Coaching is informed by 24 years of success in a Fortune 500 computer company, including 18 years as a hiring manager. Resumes, interviewing skills, career transition? Been there, done that.

It's been exciting to coach people across the globe, with the furthest being a client from Australia who met online using Skype. *I love my work*, and I can't wait to see where it all takes me next.

I'm currently living in Baltimore, Maryland, USA with my husband David.

You can read more about me and my Life & Career Coaching practice on *my professional website* (http://tinyurl.com/coach-gerry), follow me *on my*
blog (http://gettingtoclearandpresent.blogspot.com),
or email me at *GerryCoach@comcast.net*. If you think you'd enjoy one-on-one Life & Career Coaching and that it could help you reach goals much quicker, drop me a line!

Endnotes

[1] Marsha M. Linehan, *Skills Training Manual for Treating Borderline Personality Disorder* (New York: The Guilford Press, 1993), 103.

[2] Linehan, *Skills Training Manual for Treating Borderline Personality Disorder*, 177.

[3] Gina Kolatta, "After 'The Biggest Loser,' Their Bodies Fought to Regain Weight," The New York Times, 05-02-2016, *http://www.nytimes.com/2016/05/02/health/biggest-loser-weight-loss.html*

[4] "Habit Formation," Psychology Today, Viewed on 05-09-2016, *http://www.psychologytoday.com/basics/habit-formation*

[5] Charles Duhigg, *The Power of Habit: Why We Do What We Do in Life and Business* (New York: Random House, 2012), 20.

[6] Duhigg, *The Power of Habit, 20.*

[7] Duhigg, *The Power of Habit*, 49.

[8] Duhigg, *The Power of Habit*, 20.

[9] Duhigg, *The Power of Habit*, 25.

[10] Gretchen Rubin, "Stop Expecting to Change Your Habit in 21 Days: How long does it really take to change a habit?," Psychology Today, 10-21-2009, *http://www.psychologytoday.com/blog/the-happiness-project/200910/stop-expecting-change-your-habit-in-21-days*

[11] Duhigg, *The Power of Habit, 62.*

[12] Duhigg, *The Power of Habit, 84.*

[13] Duhigg, *The Power of Habit, 143-47.*

[14] Duhigg, *The Power of Habit, xiv.*

[15] Duhigg, *The Power of Habit, 109.*

[16] Duhigg, *The Power of Habit,108-9.*

[17] Duhigg, *The Power of Habit, 109.*

[18] Duhigg, *The Power of Habit, 109.*

[19] Duhigg, *The Power of Habit, 120-21.*

[20] Duhigg, *The Power of Habit, 131.*

[21] Duhigg, *The Power of Habit, 1*

[22] Duhigg, *The Power of Habit, 138-39*

[23] Duhigg, *The Power of Habit, 150-151.*

[24] Oliver Burkeman, "This Column will change your life: how long does it really take to change a habit?," The Guardian, 10-09-2009, *http://www.theguardian.com/lifeandstyle/2009/oct/10 /change-your-life-habit-28-day-rule*

[25] Oliver Burkeman, "This Column will change your life: how long does it really take to change a habit?," The Guardian, 10-09-2009,
http://www.theguardian.com/lifeandstyle/2009/oct/10/change-your-life-habit-28-day-rule

[26] Gretchen Rubin, "Stop Expecting to Change Your Habit in 21 Days: How long does it really take to change a habit?," Psychology Today, 10-21-2009,
http://www.psychologytoday.com/blog/the-happiness-project/200910/stop-expecting-change-your-habit-in-21-days

[27] Duhigg, *The Power of Habit*, 108-9.

[28] Duhigg, *The Power of Habit, 84-5.*

[29] Duhigg, *The Power of Habit, 84.*

[30] Kendra Cherry, "Theories of Motivation: A Closer Look at Some Important Theories of Motivation," About.com Psychology, Viewed on 05-09-2016,
http://psychology.about.com/od/psychologytopics/tp/theories-of-motivation.htm

[31] John L. Schinnerer, "The Power of Positive Internal Motivation," PsychCentral, Viewed on 05-09-2016, *http://psychcentral.com/lib/the-power-of-positive-internal-motivation/0001106*

[32] Kendra Cherry, "Introduction to Operant Conditioning," About.com Psychology, Viewed on 05-09-2016, *http://psychology.about.com/od/behavioralpsychology/a/introopcond.htm*

[33] "Appreciative Inquiry: Asking Powerful Questions," Viewed on 05-09-2016, https://design.umn.edu/about/intranet/documents/AppreciativeInquiry-Asking%20Powerful%20Questions.pdf

[34] William R. Miller and Stephen Rollnick, *Motivational Interviewing: Preparing People for Change* (New York: The Guilford Press, 2002), 33-42.

[35] Edward Hallowell, M.D., *Worry: Hope and Help for a Common Condition* (New York: The Random House Publishing Group, 1997), 245-49.

[36] The Chopra Well, "Mindfulness & Intention – Panel Discussion with Meditation & Mindfulness Experts – Depak Chopra," YouTube, Viewed on 05-09-2016, *https://www.youtube.com/watch?v=1a7u_5L_bi8*

[37] Daniel Simons, "selective attention test," YouTube, Viewed on 05-09-2016, *https://www.youtube.com/watch?v=vJG698U2Mvo*

[38] "The Transtheoretical Model of Behavior Change," The HABITS Lab at UMBC, Viewed on 05-09-2016, *http://habitslab.umbc.edu/the-model/*

[39] Jim Bright, "Chaos Theory of Careers Explained—Interview with Dr. Jim Bright at Vanderbilt University," YouTube, Viewed on 05-08-2016, *https://www.youtube.com/watch?v=BL2wTkgBEyk*

[40] "Definition of pivot," Financial Times Lexicon, Viewed on 05-09-2016, *http://lexicon.ft.com/term?term=pivot*

[41] "Groupon's Billion Dollar Pivot: The Incredible Story of How Utter Failure Morphed into Fortunes," Viewed on 05-09-2016, *http://www.businessinsider.com/groupon-pivot-2011-3?op=1*

[42] "I have not failed. I've just found 10,000 ways that won't work," BrainyQuote, Viewed on 05-09-2016, *http://www.brainyquote.com/quotes/quotes/t/thomas aed132683.html*

[43] Duhigg, *The Power of Habit*, xvi.

[44] "Life is What Happens To You While You're Busy Making Other Plans," Quote Investigator, Viewed on 05-08-2016, *http://quoteinvestigator.com/2012/05/06/other-plans/*

[45] "The best is the enemy of the good," BrainyQuote, Viewed on 05-08-2016, *http://www.brainyquote.com/quotes/quotes/v/voltaire 138211.html*

[46] "Fried Green Tomatoes Quotes," IMDb, Viewed on 05-09-2016, *http://www.imdb.com/title/tt0101921/quotes*

[47] Mihaly Csikszentmihalyi, *Flow: The Psychology of Optimal Experience*, (New York: Harper Perennial, 1990, 6.

[48] Jerry Jasinowski, "It's the Economy, Stupid," Huffington Post, 11-05-2015, *http://www.huffingtonpost.com/jerry-jasinowski/presidential-debates_b_8478456.html*

[49] Linehan, *Skills Training Manual for Treating Borderline Personality Disorder*, 63-9.

[50] Gerry Fisher, "Weight loss project: Meditate while you work out," "Getting to Clear and Present," Viewed on 05-09-2016, *http://gettingtoclearandpresent.blogspot.com/2014/06/weight-loss-project-meditate-while-you.html*

[51] David D. Burns, MD, *The Feeling Good Handbook* (New York: Plume, 1999), 5-7.

[52] Burns, *The Feeling Good Handbook*, 8-11.

Made in the USA
Middletown, DE
04 August 2017